The Parables of the Kingdom

The Kingdom of Heaven is Here Now, But Not Yet in Fullness

Dr. Kazumba Charles

The opinions expressed in this manuscript are solely the opinions of the author and do not represent the opinions or thoughts of the publisher. The author has represented and warranted full ownership and/or legal right to publish all the materials in this book.

The Parables of the Kingdom
The Kingdom of Heaven is Here Now, But Not Yet in Fullness
All Rights Reserved.
Copyright © 2014 Dr. Kazumba Charles
V1.0 R1.0

Cover Photo © 2014 thinkstockphotos.com. All rights reserved - used with permission.

This book may not be reproduced, transmitted, or stored in whole or in part by any means, including graphic, electronic, or mechanical without the express written consent of the publisher except in the case of brief quotations embodied in critical articles and reviews.

Unless otherwise indicated, Scripture is taken from the Holman Christian Standard Bible, copyright 1999, 2000, 2002, 2003 by Holman Bible Publishers. Used by permission.

Scripture marked ESV is taken from the Holy Bible, English Standard Version, copyright © 2001 by Crossway Bibles, a division of Good News Publishers. Used by permission. All rights reserved.

Scripture marked NLT is taken from the Holy Bible, New Living Translation, copyright © 1996. Used by permission of Tyndale House Publishers, Inc., Wheaton, IL 60189. All rights reserved.

Scripture marked Tree of Life Bible is taken from *Tree of Life Bible*, copyright © 2011. Used by permission of Destiny Image® Publishers, Shippensburg, PA.

Grateful acknowledgment is made for permission to reprint excerpts from Jeffrey L. Curry, *The Parable Discovery* (Roanoke, TX: See Again Press, 2004).

Outskirts Press, Inc.
http://www.outskirtspress.com

ISBN: 978-1-4787-4362-0

Outskirts Press and the "OP" logo are trademarks belonging to Outskirts Press, Inc.

PRINTED IN THE UNITED STATES OF AMERICA

Contents

Foreword i
Acknowledgements iii
Introduction v
1: Why Jesus Taught in Parables 1
2: The Kingdom of God 14
3: The Parable of the Sower 22
4: The Parable of the Wheat and the Weeds 27
5: The Parables of the Mustard Seed and the Yeast 31
6: The Parable of the Growing Seed 36
7: The Parables of the Hidden Treasure
   and the Priceless Pearl 39
8: The Parable of the Net 43
9: The New and Old Treasures 45
10: The Parable of the Unforgiving Servant 48
11: The Parable of the Lost Sheep 56
12: The Parable of the Lost Coin 59
13: The Parable of the Lost (Prodigal) Son 62
14: The Parable of the Day Laborers (Vineyard) 69
15: The Parable of the Two Sons 73
16: The Parable of the Wedding Banquet 76

17: The Parables of the Ten Virgins and the Talents.............81
18: The Kingdom of God has come "Near You"...................88
19: The Rule and Reign of God 97
20: A Brief Summary..114
Bibliography..131

Foreword

Dr. Kazumba Charles's book, *The Parables of the Kingdom*, inspires us to a renewed interest in the study of the parables of Jesus. As he looks at the parables from a Jewish perspective, it is like a breath of fresh air that unlocks the mysteries of the kingdom of heaven for us today. I highly recommend this book to every person who has a desire to be part of advancing the kingdom of heaven here on the earth now.

Dr. David A. Pierce
Dean, Faith Alive Bible College

Acknowledgements

With special thanks:

To God and our Lord Jesus Christ for helping me in every step of my studies and my life and for providing for me in every area.

To Pastor Brent and Barb Rudoski and Faith Alive Family Church for all the support, care, and love my family and I have received from you. I am so thankful to you for giving me an opportunity to study the Word of God in an environment full of the Spirit of the living God.

To Dr. David Pierce and Mrs. Pierce, for opening your home and your heart to my family and me and for treating us as your own children. Your encouraging words and your thoughtfulness gave me courage to study the Word of God with joy and happiness. Dr. Pierce, being around you and working with you in your garden or around the church taught me some powerful life principles that I will never forget. Yes, it is not done until it is done right; and the more I look, the more I see.

To my wife Glory for all the love, patience, encouragement, wisdom, ideals, and support you have always given to me.

To my daughters, Louriana and Briona, and my son, Joshua McCharles, for all the love you have always given to me and for putting a smile on Dad's face. I love you all.

Introduction

> Then Jesus went to all the towns and villages, teaching in their synagogues, preaching the good news of the kingdom, and healing every disease and every sickness. (Matthew 9:35)

> If I drive out demons by the Spirit of God, then the kingdom of God has come to you. (Matthew 12:28)

Jesus' message of the kingdom of heaven was a proclamation—an announcement—that God's promised Messiah had arrived. The task of the Messiah was to establish God's kingdom, and His rule and reign, here on earth. Through Jesus our Messiah, God's redemption plan was fulfilled, and His kingdom was revealed to the whole world. Jesus' kingdom parables recorded in the Gospels demonstrate the power, the rule, and the reign of God's kingdom here on earth.

Parables of the Kingdom

Parable after parable opens with the words, "The kingdom of heaven is like …" or, "The kingdom of heaven may be compared to …" or, "Then the kingdom of heaven will be like …"

or, "What is the kingdom of God like?" Such expressions highlight the message Jesus continually proclaimed. Furthermore, He challenged His disciples to go and preach the same message. He said to them, "As you go, announce this: 'The kingdom of heaven has come near'" (Matthew 10:7).

We discover the influence of the kingdom of heaven here on earth and in our own lives as we study Jesus' kingdom teaching. In this book we will examine the powerful and life-changing message of the kingdom of heaven as presented by Jesus through the parables of the kingdom. As we will see, the kingdom of heaven *is here now*; thus, a primary focus will be on the kingdom's influence here on earth and in our lives. My conviction is that no one can truly understand the nature, character, and power of the kingdom of heaven without studying Jesus' teaching on the kingdom, which encompasses some 35 percent of His words in the Gospels.

Through the parables of the kingdom of heaven, Jesus revealed God's love for the lost, real forgiveness, the rule and reign of God, the compassionate heart of God, how to enter God's kingdom, the humble beginning and growth of God's kingdom, the forcefulness of God's kingdom, the arrival of God's kingdom here on earth, and the value of the kingdom of God. The list goes on and on. Before we Christians can advance the kingdom of heaven, we first must study the teachings of Jesus concerning that kingdom. We must allow ourselves to be transformed and consumed by His message.

The focus of Jesus' preaching was God's kingdom. In fact, it is important to understand that Jesus did not preach any message other than the liberating message of the kingdom of heaven. The good news of the kingdom Jesus preached was demonstrated in power and not only in words. His message:

- Gave life to the lifeless.
- Gave hope to the hopeless.
- Turned sinners to God.
- Challenged religious communities.
- Empowered God's people.
- Demonstrated God's unconditional love.
- Demonstrated real forgiveness.
- Brought physical as well as spiritual healing to the sick.

In Matthew 4:17 we read that Jesus preached, "Repent, because the kingdom of heaven has come near!" And in Matthew 9:35 we read, "Jesus went to all the towns and villages, teaching in their synagogues, preaching the good news of the kingdom, and healing every disease and every sickness."

In the Gospel we also see that John the Baptist, the man anointed by God to prepare the way for the coming Messiah, preached only the good news of the kingdom of heaven. He preached, "Repent, because the kingdom of heaven has come near!" (Matthew 3:2).

If Jesus, our Messiah, the Son of the living God, preached only the good news of the kingdom, and John the Baptist, the man anointed and sent by God to prepare the way for the Messiah, also preached only the good news of the kingdom, then it is crucial that we pay attention to this message of the kingdom of heaven. Anything in the Bible that receives such emphasis certainly is very important and demands our attention.

Studying the message of the kingdom of heaven as proclaimed by Jesus will give us greater understanding of the nature of God and the characteristics of His kingdom. It also will help us discover how the kingdom of heaven operates and how it should influence us here on earth. When believers in

Christ truly capture the message of the kingdom of heaven, the church will begin to forcefully advance God's kingdom to the ends of the earth.

In Christ, the kingdom of heaven has arrived, though not yet in its fullness. It has arrived to influence our hearts, our nations, and our communities. This powerful kingdom has arrived to empower us to live for God, to advance its influence, and to demonstrate its mighty power and love to the ends of the earth.

What Is a Parable?

The Hebrew word for parable, *mashal,* "has a wide range of meanings. The word is stretched from its basic meaning of similarity or resemblance, to cover any type of illustration, from a proverbial saying to a fictitious story. It may refer to a proverb, riddle, anecdote, fable, or allegory."[1] One of the two Greek words translated "parable" in the New Testament is *paroimia* (appearing four times in the gospel of John), which means a proverb or a presentation. The other Greek word for parable is *parabole*, which is used fifty times in the New Testament. It means to represent or stand for something.

This more common Greek word for parable merely refers to a comparison made by placing things side by side. Jesus used parables to teach heavenly or spiritual truths by comparing them to earthly truths, or happenings in ordinary life. This method helped people grasp spiritual concepts such as the reality of the kingdom of heaven. At a basic level, a parable is a short story designed to convey a concept to be understood or a principle to be put into practice.

---

1   Brad H. Young, *The Parables* (Peabody, MA: Hendrickson, 1998), 3.

A parable defines the unknown by using what is known. The unknown God is revealed through what is known by human experience. Parables communicate a single message and urge a decision.²

---

2   Ibid.

Chapter 1

Why Jesus Taught in Parables

Mark 4:33–34 says of Jesus, "He would speak the word to them with many parables like these, as they were able to understand. And He did not speak to them without a parable. Privately, however, He would explain everything to His own disciples."

The same verse in a different version of the Bible states, "He used many such stories and illustrations to teach the people as much as they were able to understand. In fact, in his public teaching he taught only with parables, but afterward when he was alone with his disciples, he explained the meaning to them" (NLT).

Jesus frequently taught using parables to illustrate profound and divine truths. The verses cited above indicate that parables were Jesus' regular method of public teaching. Parabolic stories are easily remembered and are rich in meaning, and the Jewish people of Jesus' day were very familiar with this common form of teaching.

Why did Jesus use parables to teach His disciples the message of the kingdom? And why did He let most people wonder about the meaning of His parables while explaining the meaning only to His disciples? In Mark 4:10, Jesus' disciples privately asked Him about the meaning of the parables He taught publicly. He answered them in verses 11 and 12:

> "You are permitted to understand the secret about the Kingdom of God. But I am using these stories to conceal everything about it from outsiders, so that the Scriptures might be fulfilled: 'They see what I do, but they don't perceive its meaning. They hear my words, but they don't understand. So they will not turn from their sins and be forgiven.'" (NLT)

In Matthew 13, Jesus' disciples were wondering again why Jesus spoke in parables to the crowds that had gathered around Him on the shore of the sea.

> Then the disciples came up and asked Him, "Why do you speak to them in parables?" He answered them, "Because the secrets of the kingdom of heaven have been given for you to know, but it has not been given to them . . . But whoever does not have, even what he has will be taken away from him. For this reason I speak to them in parables, because looking they do not see, and hearing they do not listen or understand." (Matthew 13:10–13)

Here is the answer to why Jesus used parables as his teaching tool. He explained the parables to his disciples, but those who had continually rejected the good news of the kingdom were left in their spiritual blindness to wonder as to his meaning.

The Parables of the Kingdom

In Matthew 13, Jesus clearly distinguished between those who had been given "ears to hear" (verses 9, 43) and those who persisted in unbelief—ever hearing but never actually perceiving and always learning but never able to acknowledge the truth (verses 13–15).

The disciples had been given the gift of spiritual discernment by which the things of the Spirit were made clear to them. Because of their acceptance of the good news of the kingdom Jesus proclaimed, they were given more and more truth and revelation.

Through the parables of the kingdom, Jesus revealed the secrets, or mysteries, of the kingdom of God—but only to His disciples. He revealed the mysteries of God to His disciples because they belonged to Him. Those who do not yet participate in the kingdom of heaven here on earth cannot understand the mysteries of the kingdom of heaven. Accepting Jesus Christ as our Lord and Savior and submitting to His rule and reign makes the mysteries of the Lord's (Yahweh's) kingdom plain and understandable.

In Mark 4:10–12, Jesus distinguished between two audiences: "You" (the Twelve, or the disciples) to whom revelation had been given by God, and "those outside." Both groups heard the parables, but only the insiders—the disciples—learned the secret. "Secret" is literally "mystery." The secret relates to the kingdom of God, which Jesus came to announce (Mark 1:15).

First Corinthians 2:14 tells us the unbeliever "does not welcome what comes from God's Spirit, because it is foolishness to him; he is not able to know it since it is evaluated spiritually." A person who has not yet accepted the influence of the kingdom of God in his life cannot understand the "mysteries" of the kingdom of God. Mysteries related to such things as Christ's power, love, peace, life, and joy cannot be understood without being a disciple of Jesus. The mysteries of the kingdom of heaven are revealed only to disciples of Jesus (Yeshua).

Why Should We Study the Parables of Jesus?

Jesus' kingdom parables reveal the mysteries of the kingdom of heaven. These mysteries center on God's divine power and authority. When we accept the rule and reign of God in our lives, God gives us the power, authority, and privilege to become His children or subjects.

If we are to understand the true nature, character, and power of God, we must study the parables of Jesus. Studying His parables in light of Jewish culture and background will open our understanding of the kingdom of heaven and help us grasp how it should affect our lives. The Jewish background of the parables provides the key for understanding the good news of the kingdom. The core meaning of Jesus' parables is discovered in the rich heritage of Jewish *Haggadah;* that is, giving an illustration to drive home a higher theological truth.[3]

An understanding of Jesus' parables is essential to understanding the kingdom of heaven. The parables open our eyes to the activities of the kingdom of heaven and teach us the principles of God. Parables are key to advancing the kingdom of heaven here on earth.

In summary, then, here are the reasons we should study the parables of Jesus:

- To understand the parables of Jesus is to understand Jesus' purpose and mission here on earth. Jesus' main purpose was to bring God's kingdom and power to the people and for the people. He came to preach the good

---

[3] Young, *The Parables*, 7–8.

The Parables of the Kingdom

news of the kingdom to the poor, to bind up the brokenhearted, to proclaim freedom for the captives, and to release people from the prison of darkness (Isaiah 61:1). Only the kingdom of heaven has legitimate power to set people free; nothing else does.

- The parables of Jesus help us understand the divine nature, authority, and character of God.
- The parables of Jesus help us understand the message of the kingdom of heaven that Jesus preached and thus help us to preach the same message to the nations of the world.
- To understand the parables of Jesus is to discover the power and the effect of the kingdom of heaven here on earth.
- The parables teach us to have patience, love, mercy, and forgiveness.

The Ancient Jewish Teaching Technique

Let's look at the ancient Jewish teaching technique known as the *Mashal-plus-Nimshal* method, which is the method Jesus employed throughout Matthew's gospel. In doing so, I want to quote extensively from Jeffrey Curry's *The Parable Discovery*.

In modern day terms, mashal + nimshal would be interpreted as parable + explanation. Each ancient Jewish parable ... by definition, design, and intent, had a real-life target (the nimshal). Here is an example of a typical ancient Jewish parable, the mashal and nimshal, or the parable + its real life target.

Dr. Kazumba Charles

Mashal (Parable)	**Nimshal** (Real-life target)
Rabbi Abba bar Kahana said: It is like a king who married a woman and wrote her a large marriage settlement. He wrote her: So many bridal-chambers I am building for you; so much jewelry I make for you; so much gold and silver I give you. Then he left her for many years and journeyed to the provinces. Her neighbors used to taunt her and say to her: Hasn't your husband abandoned you? Go! Marry another man. She would weep and sigh, and afterward she would enter her bridal-chamber and read her marriage settlement and sigh [with relief]. Many years and days later the king returned. He said to her: I am amazed that you have waited for me all these years! She replied: My master, O king! If not for the large wedding settlement you wrote me, my neighbors long ago would have led me astray.	Rabbi Abba bar Kahana said: It is like a king who married a woman and wrote her a large marriage settlement. He wrote her: So many bridal-chambers I am building for you; so much jewelry I make for you; so much gold and silver I give you. Then he left her for many years and journeyed to the provinces. Her neighbors used to taunt her and say to her: Hasn't your husband abandoned you?

The Parables of the Kingdom

For teaching purposes, the parable by itself was insufficient. It would be very difficult, if not impossible, to properly understand the mashal by itself, as given above. To rightly understand it, the nimshal . . . had to be introduced to its hearers. Neither was it a coincidence that Jesus' own disciples failed to understand the parables (mashal without its nimshal, or 'real-life' target) that their Master first spoke (Matthew 13:36). The ancient Hebrew parable was a fictional story that was meant to teach a particular truth or a set of truths (principles) about a real life occurrence, but it was only when the parable (Matthew 13:3-8) and the explanation (Matthew13:18-23) were given together that they actually made sense. . . . Without the Author of the parables' help, the student (13:36) usually could not figure out the meaning of the parable by itself . . . at least not correctly, and this was by design. The ancient Jewish parables were enigmatic and mysterious, and intentionally so. They were designed to create a dependent teaching relationship between the master and the student. The meshalim (plural of mashal) were not independent statements of truth. They required the nimshal (whether revealed or implied) to communicate their intended meaning. . . . Jesus gave the multitude only the first half of the equation when He stood on the seashore that day (Matthew 13:1-50), and then promptly admitted to His disciples that He did that so the parables' meanings would remain concealed (13:11). If the multitudes and the disciples couldn't understand His parables without an explanation, should we feel bad if we can't?[4]

---

[4] Jeffrey L. Curry, *The Parable Discovery* (Roanoke, TX: See Again Press, 2004). Quotations are taken by permission from excerpts at www.theparablediscovery.com.

No, we need not feel bad, because most parables are not easy to understand without an explanation. However, focusing on the target of any parable can help us understand the meaning of the parable.

Jesus gave the parable without the explanation, or the mashal without t*he nimshal,* the real target. **The fact that He supplied only the parables, in order to conceal their actual meanings, should reveal to [us] that an explanation was absolutely necessary.** Furthermore, it was no coincidence that when Jesus did give the explanations, it was only to His disciples. Those who did not get an explanation remained in the dark, while those who did, achieved understanding. You see, to obtain the explanations required a relationship . . . a discipleship relationship. It's true that Jesus didn't reveal His wisdom for all to hear. . . . Why? Because otherwise, if He had, there would have been no need for a relationship, or a **discipleship** as the first century Hebrews would have called it. Yet, even though Jesus withheld the explanations of the parables from those on the seashore that day, they still could have obtained the explanations for themselves . . . but only for a price. That price was discipleship. To obtain the explanations of the parables, or the mysteries of the kingdom, they had to follow The Teacher; they had to become a disciple of His. Jesus withheld information regarding the kingdom from the multitudes . . . to draw those interested in the Kingdom of Heaven into a relationship with Him. Parables were the staple of the first century sage . . . they were the teaching staple of Jesus Christ. To understand His parables today, we must first find their explanations.

The key to finding the 'explanation,' or nimshal [real target] for each of the kingdom parables (13:1-50) lies in the literary organization of the book of Matthew (i.e., the explanations for each parable are revealed by the overall literary organization of the book of Matthew, or when one understands Matthew's organizational pattern, he or she can find each and every explanation Matthew left for each of the parables. [Matthew, emulating his Master, hid the explanations of the parables just like Jesus did when He first spoke them.])[5]

Jesus' Method of Teaching

When Jesus began to teach by using parables, He was using a method of story-telling that coincided with Middle Eastern thought patterns. The mind-set of the average Palestinian in the first-century was not all systematized in tight patterns of deductive and inductive Aristotelian logic. They were simple people, who often used the language of imagery and idioms, which employed word-pictures based on known agricultural, vocational, social, political, and religious customs.[6]

While Jesus used a variety of teaching methods chosen for the situation and to meet the needs of His hearers, one of

---

5   Curry, *The Parable Discovery*..
6   James A. Fowler, "Parables of the Kingdom," Christ in You Ministries, http://www.christinyou.net/pages/paroking.html

His favorite methods of teaching was through telling stories, or parables. However, it is very important to understand that parables are not just nice stories; they are powerful illustrations that illuminate the characteristics of God. Parables make the message of the kingdom of heaven practical. Jesus used them to reach people and teach them at a variety of levels. As we listen to the parables of Jesus, we are encouraged to apply the truths they teach to our daily lives.

The Purpose of the Parables

As previously stated, Jesus' use of parables in His teaching had two distinct purposes:

1. To reveal the truth to those who were willing to hear and believe.
2. To conceal the truth from those who willingly rejected the truth because of their calloused hearts (Matthew 13:15).

In regard to the revelation of truth, the parables focus on God and His kingdom. In doing so, they reveal what kind of God He is, by what principles He works, and what He expects of humanity. Because of their focus on the kingdom, some of the parables reveal many aspects of Jesus' mission as well, as we see, for example, in the parable of the wicked tenants in Matthew 21:33–41.

Jesus often used parables to teach His followers because parables can powerfully drive home a life-changing and transforming point. Parables in both the Gospels and in rabbinic literature had an instructive purpose. Jesus' parables instruct us to follow the ways of God's kingdom. They introduce

The Parables of the Kingdom

the mysteries, or the power, of the kingdom of heaven to mankind.

Jesus' parables also give His disciples insight into how the kingdom of heaven operates and how people should respond to it. As we go through the parables of Jesus, we will see the power of the kingdom of heaven convincingly demonstrated and revealed in a simple, yet forceful and life-changing way.

We will also see two different aspects of the kingdom. In some cases Jesus referred to the "present" aspect of the kingdom of heaven, and at other times He referred to the "future" aspect of the kingdom. The kingdom should not be confined to the end times alone; the kingdom of heaven is here now, even though it is not yet revealed in its fullness. Yes, in the future, the fullness of God's kingdom will be revealed; but that does not mean the rule and reign of the kingdom of God is not yet in operation here on earth.

In Matthew 12:28–29, Jesus announced the arrival of the kingdom of heaven here on earth:

> If I drive out demons by the Spirit of God, then the kingdom of God has come to you. How can someone enter a strong man's house and steal his possessions unless he first ties up the strong man? Then he can rob his house.

The kingdom of heaven has arrived, invading Satan's kingdom and binding him. Satan, who was once a strong man, has been defeated. Jesus' power to cast out demons proved that the kingdom of God has arrived and has overthrown Satan's kingdom. Each time we see people healed, marriages transformed, hard hearts softened, and people come to the Lord, we should acknowledge that the kingdom of heaven has arrived.

During His earthly ministry, Jesus demonstrated the full force and power of the kingdom of heaven here on earth by healing many sick people and by setting the captives free. The rule and reign of the kingdom of heaven has arrived. It is here and is already operating within the hearts of men and women who have received Jesus Christ. When people accept Jesus into their lives, they are simply accepting and allowing the rule and reign of God in their lives, and that means King Jesus must rule and reign in their lives.

In the simplest terms, the parables of Jesus reveal the mystery of the kingdom of heaven to mankind here on earth and demonstrate its power and authority. They show that the kingdom of heaven is undefeatable, unshakable, and immovable. Indeed, no earthly kingdom can be compared to the kingdom of heaven. The kingdom of God is God's government, and He rules over the nations and over His people righteously and justly.

In Revelation 21:3–4, God revealed to John, in a vision, what His kingdom will look like when it arrives in its fullness. John wrote:

> I heard a loud shout from the throne, saying, "Look, the home of God is now among his people! He will live with them, and they will be his people. God himself will be with them. He will remove all of their sorrows, and there will be no more death or sorrow or crying or pain. For the old world and its evils are gone forever." (NLT)

In the kingdoms of the world, we see death, sorrow, pain, and tears in the lives of people. However, in God's kingdom none of these things exist. God's home (presence) will be

The Parables of the Kingdom

among His people, and He Himself will live with them. The earth will be new, the old earth will disappear, and instead of God's people going up, God will come down once again to live among His people.

Chapter 2

The Kingdom of God

What Is the Kingdom of God?

God's kingdom, sometimes referred to as the kingdom of Christ, the kingdom of heaven, or simply the kingdom, is mentioned more than one hundred times in the New Testament. There are four references to the "kingdom of God" in Matthew (the variation "*kingdom of heaven*" is used another thirty-four times), fourteen in Mark, thirty-two in Luke, and two in John. In order to understand what the "kingdom of God" or "kingdom of heaven" really means, we need to turn to the Hebrew word that is translated "kingdom" to get the big picture of the kingdom of God Jesus preached.

Definition of a Kingdom

The word *kingdom* can be defined as a territory in which a king rules over his subjects, or a domain in which something is dominant. Jesus' kingdom is different from earthly kingdoms in that it is not a kingdom of this world (John 18:36). It is not a physical kingdom with geographical boundaries as earthly

The Parables of the Kingdom

kingdoms are. Neither is it a kingdom that can be seen with human eyes. Our eyes can see only the actions, power, effects, and dominion of God's kingdom here on earth operating in the lives of believers.[7]

The Hebrew words for "kingdom of heaven," *malkuth ha shamayim* (Mah-Koot ha Shah-MYeem), may sound like they are referring to a place or a government of some kind. However, this ancient Hebrew phrase, which is an idiom common in rabbinic teaching, actually describes the actions and dominion of a king.

Malkuth means "kingdom," while *shamayim* means "sky" or "heavens." The word *heaven* in the expression "kingdom of heaven" refers to God and not to a place. So the "kingdom of heaven" simply refers to how God reigns and those over whom He reigns.

The Greek word for kingdom used in the New Testament, *basileia*, also refers to rank, authority, and sovereignty exercised by a king. Just as an earthly king exercises his sovereign authority over his people, God exercises His authority over anybody who belongs to His kingdom. Whenever Jesus spoke of the kingdom of heaven, He was not referring to a geographical boundary but to God's rule, authority, and sovereignty.

Through Jesus Christ, God revealed His authority, dominion, and power over sickness, death, and demons here on earth. Signs and wonders accompanied Jesus to prove this dominion and power of God's kingdom over everything.

Definition of God's Kingdom

In the simplest terms, we can say that the kingdom of God is the rule of God over us (His subjects). God's kingdom is

[7] Paraphrased from Michael Graham, "Parables of the Kingdom," Michael Graham Ministries, http://www.michaelgrahamministries.org/mark/mark16.html

invisible to the natural eye but very visible to the spiritual eye, because the kingdom of God is within every believer in Christ (Luke 17:20–21). Wherever the Lord Jesus Christ reigns, whether in an individual life, a nation, or a group, the kingdom of God is there. God's kingdom exists in the spiritual realm because God is Spirit (John 4:24).

Jesus said that no one can see, perceive, or understand the kingdom of God unless he or she is born again, or born of the Spirit (John 3:3). And no one can enter the kingdom of God unless he or she is born of water, a symbol of the Word of God (Ephesians 5:26; 1 Peter 1:23), and of the Spirit (John 3:5). The kingdom of God consists of all (subjects) who have surrendered themselves to the Lord Jesus Christ and made Him King and Lord of their lives.

The biblical ideal of the kingdom of God is deeply rooted in the Hebrew Scriptures (Old Testament) and is grounded in the truth that there is one eternal, living God who has revealed Himself to mankind.

A Spiritual Kingdom, Not a Military Kingdom

At the time of Christ's earthly ministry, the Roman Empire was at its peak, and people had a very visible example or ideal of how a kingdom looked and operated. Indeed, the Jews of Jesus' day expected God to send a visible, military kingdom that would overpower and overthrow their enemies who had oppressed them for so long. They were not prepared to see a nonmilitary, spiritual kingdom announced and demonstrated by Jesus Christ.

Jesus preached that the kingdom of heaven is at hand, or near, or "has come." Jesus' mission was to restore man to his rightful place in the kingdom of heaven, not in an earthly kingdom. Thus, He called on people to repent because the kingdom of God had arrived. Many who expected the arrival of a military kingdom opposed and rejected Christ, yet those whose spiritual eyes were opened by the Spirit of God accepted and received Him.

Is the Kingdom of Heaven Different from the Kingdom of God?

Before we finally get into the parables of Jesus, let's take a quick look at the expressions *kingdom of heaven* and *kingdom of God*. Is there any difference between these two expressions? Is the kingdom of heaven different from the kingdom of God?

Some try to make a distinction between the kingdom of heaven and the kingdom of God, but a quick comparison of their use in the Gospels indicates that the two terms refer to the same thing and are not at all different from each other. Compare the following verses in the Gospels.

Matthew 4:17: "From then on Jesus began to preach, 'Repent, because the kingdom of heaven has come near!'"

Mark 1:14–15: "After John was arrested, Jesus went to Galilee, preaching the good news of God: 'The time is fulfilled, and the kingdom of God has come near. Repent and believe in the good news!'"

Matthew 5:3: "Blessed are the poor in spirit, because the kingdom of heaven is theirs."

Luke 6:20: "Then looking up at His disciples, He said: 'Blessed are you who are poor, because the kingdom of God is yours.'"

Matthew 13:31: "He presented another parable to them: 'The kingdom of heaven is like a mustard seed that a man took and sowed in his field.'"

Mark 4:30–31: "And He said: 'How can we illustrate the kingdom of God, or what parable can we use to describe it?' It's like a mustard seed …"

The parallel verses above demonstrate that the kingdom of heaven and the kingdom of God are equivalent. When Jesus uses "the kingdom of heaven" in one verse and in another verse uses "the kingdom of God," He is not talking about two different kingdoms.

Neither are Matthew, Mark, and Luke talking about two separate kingdoms. There is only one kingdom of God. Different expressions by the Gospel writers should not cause us to think the kingdom of heaven is totally different from the kingdom of God. God has only one camp, which may be called either the kingdom of heaven or the kingdom of God.

Why, then, were different expressions used in different contexts? Matthew used the expression "kingdom of heaven" almost exclusively, while the other Gospel writers used the phrase "kingdom of God." Most Bible scholars believe that because Matthew wrote his gospel to the Jews, he chose to use the phrase "kingdom of heaven" because of the Jews' reluctance to use the name of God, out of reverence for Him.

Because of some Jews' misconceptions of the coming kingdom, many of them anticipated a physical kingdom, yet *heaven* (literally, *heavens*) would emphasize a spiritual kingdom. So our first observation is that any effort to distinguish between the kingdom of heaven and the kingdom of God is really without warrant.

What the Kingdom of Heaven Is Not

The Kingdom of Heaven Is Not the Church

Many people tend to think the kingdom of God or kingdom of heaven is the church. The church is not the kingdom of God. There are several clear distinctions between the church and the kingdom of God. The terms *church* and *kingdom* are never used interchangeably in Scripture, as the *kingdom of God* and the *kingdom of heaven* are. Of the 114 occurrences of the word *church* (Greek, *ekklesia*), it is never used with the kingdom. The kingdom of God is the rule and reign of God. The church is an important part of God's kingdom, but it is not the kingdom of God that Jesus proclaimed.

The full arrival of God's kingdom will occur when the King who rules the kingdom, Jesus Christ, arrives in power and glory at His second coming. This makes it plain that the entity called the church is not the kingdom of which the Bible speaks. Furthermore, it is very clear, according to Scripture, that the apostles preached the kingdom of God (Acts 8:12; 19:8; 28:23); and one cannot substitute the church for the kingdom in these passages.

It must be said, however, that there is a strong and

unbreakable relationship between the church and the kingdom of heaven. The church is made up of those who are born anew and submit to Christ's rulership in their lives. Thus, those who are part of Christ's church are also part of His kingdom, and they are a part of it both now and later when He returns.

The church is a powerful and God-ordained instrument that Jesus uses to demonstrate to mankind here on earth the power, character, and nature of His kingdom. The church consists of people who have accepted and allowed the rule and reign of God's kingdom in their lives. The church is a light to the world, even if it has not yet lived up to God's expectation because of mankind's spiritual ups and downs.

The church is an important part of God's kingdom here on earth, and nothing can change that. It is a vehicle God uses to empower, strengthen, and build His people as they spread the message of His kingdom and wait for the full arrival of that kingdom. Robert T. Woodworth puts it this way: "The church is the body of Christ, made up of believers. It is not temporal nor material, but spiritual and eternal. The kingdom of God is the application of a heavenly principle to human government on earth."[8]

*The Kingdom of Heaven Is Not
an Apocalyptic Realm or End-Time Event*

Many people think the kingdom of heaven is a future, end-time event. The kingdom of heaven is *not* an end-time event; it is simply God's reign, His authority to rule over the nations and over His created people. The kingdom of God is God's conquest, through Jesus Christ, of His enemies: sin, Satan, and death. The kingdom of heaven comes in stages. It was foretold

---

8   Robert T. Woodworth, "The Kingdom Is Not the Church," *The Kingdom Digest,* April 1978. http://ensignmessage.com/archives/notchurch.html (accessed February 1, 2013).

The Parables of the Kingdom

by the Jewish prophets as an everlasting, mighty, and righteous reign involving the nation of Israel and its coming King, the Messiah.

The kingdom came humbly through the virgin birth of the Son of God, and it exists today as a powerful "mystery" in the hearts of all the believers in Christ. It is forcefully advancing today, and at the second coming of Christ, the kingdom of heaven will fully arrive in the splendor of God's glory and in power; and every knee shall at that moment bow before the King and tremble.

Christ will rule and reign physically on earth. Then He will deliver the kingdom to the Father, having finally put away sin, death, and Satan—who will be cast into the lake of fire (hell).

Now that we have established the background, meaning, and purpose of the parables, let's move forward and take an interesting journey into the powerful teachings of Jesus about the kingdom of heaven as illustrated in the parables. Studying the kingdom parables will help us understand the effect, power, and influence of the kingdom of God, both in our lives personally and here on earth.

In this study we are going to focus mainly on the parables of Jesus that are recorded in the gospel of Matthew, but we will also examine a few parables that are recorded in the gospels of Luke and Mark. The reason we will begin with the parables recorded in the book of Matthew is that Matthew gives us more details and explanation in the parables of Jesus than any of the other gospel writers.

Chapter 3

The Parable of the Sower

In Matthew 13:1–8, Jesus addressed a large crowd of people and told them this parable:

> Consider the sower who went out to sow. As he was sowing, some seeds fell along the path, and the birds came and ate them up. Others fell on rocky ground, where there wasn't much soil, and they sprang up quickly since the soil wasn't deep. But when the sun came up they were scorched, and since they had no root, they withered. Others fell among thorns, and the thorns came up and choked them. Still others fell on good ground and produced a crop: some 100, some 60, and some 30 times what was sown.

This parable is important to us because it sets the tone for all the parables that immediately follow. Also, this parable is one of the few where Jesus' explanation to His disciples is given.

Context

In the Jewish culture, farmers walked through their fields

The Parables of the Kingdom

broadly scattering seed by hand across their land, knowing that a large amount of seed would not bear fruit. Another member of the family would follow the sower closely and plow the seed under. Many of the seeds were eaten by birds as they fell on footpaths; others landed in shallow soil with a stratum of rock beneath; and still other seeds fell at the fringes of the property among thornbushes the farmers used to build small cooking fires. Still, the seed was broadcast widely, and some found good soil and yielded a crop.

Jesus Explains the Parable of the Sower

- In Matthew 13:18–23, Jesus explained the parable of the sower privately to His disciples. He made the following points:
- "When anyone hears the word about the kingdom and doesn't understand it, the evil one comes and snatches away what was sown in his heart. This is the one sown along the path" (verse 19).
- "And the one sown on rocky ground—this is one who hears the word and immediately receives it with joy. Yet he has no root in himself, but is short-lived. When pressure or persecution comes because of the word, immediately he stumbles" (verses 20–21).
- "Now the one sown among the thorns—this is one who hears the word, but the worries of this age and the seduction of wealth choke the word, and it becomes unfruitful" (verse 22).
- "But the one sown on the good ground—this is one who hears and understands the word, who does bear fruit and yields: some 100, some 60, some 30 times what was sown" (verse 23).

The parable of the sower concerns a farmer who scatters seed, which falls on four different types of ground. The hard ground by the wayside prevents the seed from sprouting at all, and the seed becomes nothing more than bird food. The stony ground provides enough soil for the seeds to germinate, and they begin to grow; but because there is no depth of earth, the plants do not take root and soon wither in the sun. The thorny ground allows the seed to grow, but the competing thorns choke the life out of the plants. The good ground receives the seed and produces much fruit.

It seems clear that Jesus was playing this out as He was speaking (as a sower going forth to sow). He was talking about a sower, and yet *He* is that sower who went forth and scattered seeds (the word of the kingdom) on four different types of ground and got four different results or responses. The first three grounds did not produce fruit (or respond well) because the soil was not good enough to support life. Only the fourth ground was good and produced the fruit.

In this parable, Jesus laid down a scriptural principle: All fruit production in the kingdom of God comes as a result of people receiving and properly responding to the good news of the kingdom and holding fast to it until God's power and presence are manifested in their lives. Life begins in a seed, but the seed first must be planted in the soil and "die" before it can bring forth life (fruit).

Jesus' emphasis in this parable is on the various types of soil. The kind of soil in which a farmer plants his seed will determine the growth of his crops. If the soil is good, the seed will produce good and healthy fruits; but if the soil is not good, the seed will produce nothing. Usually when a farmer puts his seed into the ground and nothing comes up, it is not the seed's fault but the ground's (soil).

The Parables of the Kingdom

All the seed Jesus sows is good, but the parable of the sower shows there are various responses to it, and the responses determine the ultimate outcome. Jesus' explanation of the parable of the sower (Matthew 13:18-23) highlights four different responses to the Word of God. The seed, first of all, is "the Word about the kingdom."

1. The hard ground represents people who have hardened their hearts toward the Word of God. They hear His Word but do not understand it, and Satan plucks the message away, keeping the heart dull and preventing the Word from making an impression.
2. The stony ground pictures a person who professes delight with the Word, but his heart is not changed; and when trouble arises, his so-called faith quickly disappears.
3. The thorny ground depicts one who seems to receive the Word but whose heart is full of the love of riches, pleasures, and the things of this world. These things take his time and attention away from the Word, and he ends up having no time for it.
4. The good ground portrays the one who hears, understands, and receives the Word and then allows the Word to accomplish its purpose in his life. The person represented by the "good ground" is the only one of the four who is truly a disciple of Jesus, because salvation's proof is fruit (Matthew 3:7–8; 7:15–20).

God the Father has sown the Seed for His activities and purposes here on earth. The seed of His divine activity is the incarnate manifestation of the Word of God, Jesus Christ (John 1:1,14). The Seed, Christ, was planted in the soil of this world. He was covered up. He disappeared, He died, and He rose again to life (John 12:24).

The heart is the human soil from which good or bad comes. A person's response to the good news of the kingdom (the word of God) is determined by the condition of that person's heart. This is why Proverbs 4:23 tells us to guard our hearts above all else.

Finally, the parable of the sower teaches us that God's kingdom has not yet come fully in power and great glory. Instead, at the present time, it resides in the hearts of willing believers and is resisted by many. Many people around the world have heard the good news or message of the kingdom of God; some have responded to it in faith, while many others have rejected it. Faithful men and women of God have preached and continue to preach the gospel of Jesus Christ to people around the world. In some cases the gospel has fallen on good soil, while in others it has fallen on unfruitful soil. And so it will continue until Christ returns.

Chapter 4

The Parable of the Wheat and the Weeds

In Matthew 13:26–30, Jesus presented another kingdom parable after He had just explained the parable of the sower to the disciples. In the parable of the wheat and weeds (tares), He compared the kingdom of heaven to a man who sowed good seed in his field. However, while people were sleeping, his enemy came, sowed weeds among the wheat, and left.

> When the plants sprouted and produced grain, then the weeds also appeared. The landowner's slaves came to him and said, "Master, didn't you sow good seed in your field? Then where did the weeds come from?" "An enemy did this!" he told them. "So, do you want us to go and gather them up?" the slaves asked him. "No," he said. "When you gather up the weeds, you might also uproot the wheat with them. Let both grow together until the harvest. At harvest time I'll tell the reapers: Gather the weeds first and tie them in bundles to burn them, but store the wheat in my barn."

As noted by Craig Keener, the weeds in this parable are identified as *darnel* by both Jewish scholars and Christian theologians. Darnel is related to wheat and resembles it during the early stages of growth, but it is a poisonous weed. When wheat and darnel grow together, their root systems become intertwined as the plants mature. This makes it difficult to uproot the weeds without damaging the wheat. Such a willful attempt to destroy someone's wheat crop by sowing darnel was a heinous act. The fact that Roman law prohibited sowing darnel in another person's field tells us that Jesus' parable was not unrealistic.[9]

The thing in this parable that we need to capture is that the young weeds and the young blades of wheat look the same and cannot be distinguished until they are grown and ready for harvest. This is the primary picture Jesus was trying to convey in the parable of the wheat and the weeds.

In Matthew 13:36, Jesus' disciples came to Him and said, "Explain the parable of the weeds in the field to us." He explained the parable to them in verses 37 through 43, saying,

> The One who sows the good seed is the Son of Man; the field is the world; and the good seed—these are the sons of the kingdom. The weeds are the sons of the evil one, and the enemy who sowed them is the Devil. The harvest is the end of the age, and the harvesters are angels. Therefore, just as the weeds are gathered and burned in the fire, so it will be at the end of the age. The Son of Man will send out His angels, and they will gather from His kingdom everything that causes sin and those guilty of lawlessness. They will throw them into the blazing furnace where there will be weeping and gnashing of

---

9   Craig Keener, *Matthew* (Downers Grove, IL: InterVarsity Press, 1997), 242.

The Parables of the Kingdom

teeth. Then the righteous will shine like the sun in their Father's kingdom. Anyone who has ears should listen!

The parable of the weeds among the wheat provides an idea of what the kingdom of God is like. In His explanation of the parable, Christ declared that He Himself, the Son of Man, is the sower. He spreads His redeemed seed, true believers, in the field of the world. Through His grace, Christians bear the fruit of the Spirit (Galatians 5:22–23).

In the agricultural society of Christ's time, farmers depended on the size and quality of their crops. An enemy sowing weeds in their wheat fields would severely damage their businesses. Without modern weed killers, what could a wise farmer do in such a situation? Instead of destroying the wheat in an attempt to remove the tares, the landowner in this parable wisely decided to wait until the harvest. After harvesting the whole field, the weeds could be separated and burned and the remaining wheat stored in the barn.

This parable occurs in the context of a whole series of parables Jesus told in Matthew 13 about the kingdom of God. What is the kingdom of God like? To what may it be compared? How does God rule? From this parable, we learn that patience and tolerance are important in the kingdom of God. God's patience is amazing, and no one can fully understand or comprehend it. He is not in a hurry to uproot the weeds (sinners) but *is* patiently waiting for His appointed time (harvesttime) to separate the weeds from the wheat.

The central theme of the parable of the wheat and weeds is that God's people for now must live side by side with unbelievers (weeds), people who are under Satan's influence. However, the time will come—and it is fast approaching—when the angels of Jesus, the Harvester, will separate the weeds from the wheat. For now, His people must demonstrate to the world how to be good and healthy plants (wheat) influenced by the kingdom of heaven, and they must snatch as many others as they can from the kingdom of Satan (Jude verse 23).

Chapter 5

The Parables of the Mustard Seed and the Yeast

He presented another parable to them: "The kingdom of heaven is like a mustard seed that a man took and sowed in his field. It's the smallest of all the seeds, but when grown, it's taller than the vegetables and becomes a tree, so that the birds of the sky come and nest in its branches."

He told them another parable: "The kingdom of heaven is like yeast that a woman took and mixed into 50 pounds of flour until it spread through all of it." (Matthew 13:31–33)

While Jesus spoke these two brief parables to the "crowds" (Matthew 13:34), they were especially designed to teach the disciples about the nature of the kingdom of God Jesus was proclaiming (verse 10). The disciples had their own ideas about the kingdom, which centered on a messianic conquest of the Roman oppressors and a restoration of David's throne. They had little understanding of the true nature of the kingdom of

God, of which they were ambassadors-in-training. The parables of the mustard seed and of the leaven (or yeast) were meant to give them a new perspective.

The Parable of the Mustard Seed

The parable of the mustard seed is recorded in all three of the Synoptic Gospels (Matthew, Mark, and Luke). However, the gospel of Matthew provides us with the most peripheral information, as it includes one parable before and one after the mustard seed parable, each giving instruction on the same subject: the kingdom of heaven.

In the land of Israel, the tiny mustard seed was well known. It is about the size of a grain of salt, one of the tiniest seeds in the whole world;[10] yet it grows into a shrub or tree with branches in which birds are able to find rest. In Luke 17:6 Jesus used the mustard seed to describe the tiniest amount of faith.

> "Mustard" is usually identified as *Sinapis nigr,* "black mustard," which grows to a shrub about 4 feet high, but occasionally can grow to 15 feet high, and would qualify as a tree. Three varieties of mustard were grown in gardens because of their aromatic seeds. Jesus mentions the growth, but the main emphasis seems to be on the beginning (very small) and the end (very large).[11]

The remarkable contrast between the small beginnings of the mustard seed and the final, large mustard plant earned the tiny seed proverbial status in Judaism. The nation of Israel

---
10   Brad H. Young, *Jesus the Jewish Theologian* (Grand Rapids: Baker Academic, 1995), 78.
11   Ralph F. Wilson, *JesusWalk: Disciple Lessons from Luke's Gospel* (Loomis, CA: JesusWalk Publications, 2010), excerpted quote from lesson 61 online at http://www.jesuswalk.com/lessons/13_18-21.htm

The Parables of the Kingdom

in Jesus' day was not prepared for an insignificant beginning to the kingdom of God. This can be traced back to the time the Israelites had returned to the land from exile in Babylon. Zechariah 4:10 says, "For who scorns the day of small things? These seven eyes of the LORD, which scan throughout the whole earth, will rejoice when they see the plumb line in Zerubbabel's hand." The Israelites had returned from exile to rebuild the temple, but the work had been hindered and stalled. The people were discouraged by the small and poor beginning to the rebuilding of the temple, and many were disheartened when they realized how long it might take to accomplish the task. The Lord told them not to despise these small beginnings. In Zechariah 4:6, the Lord told Zerubbabel that it was not by force or strength but by the Spirit of the Lord that the temple would be rebuilt. Nothing would stand in Zerubbabel's way. Even a mighty mountain would become a level plain before him! And when Zerubbabel set the final stone of the temple in place, the people would shout, "Grace, grace to it!" (Zechariah 4:7).

Jesus used the parables of the mustard seed and the yeast to show that while the kingdom of heaven has small beginnings, it will grow and produce great results. Jesus was teaching that like a mustard seed, the kingdom of heaven began as something small and seemingly insignificant, but it will grow to be very large. The parable of the growing seed, discussed later, shows *how* God causes His kingdom to grow; the parable of the mustard seed describes the *extent* to which it will grow.

The Parable of the Yeast (Leaven)

The parable of the yeast, or leaven, is very succinct: "The kingdom of heaven is like yeast that a woman took and mixed into 50 pounds of flour until it spread through all of it" (Matthew 13:33).

Yeast is a fungus that is used in baking to lighten and expand dough. The significant thing about yeast is its power, influence, and permeating effect. In the Bible it often symbolizes evil and its pervasive corruption, but this is not always the case. It also is used to symbolize good. In Matthew 13:33, Jesus used the positive effect of leaven upon dough to provide a powerful illustration of the influence and impact of the kingdom of heaven here on earth. Thus, the yeast here does not symbolize evil, for the kingdom of heaven is good, life-giving, and empowering.

The parable of the yeast goes hand in hand with the parable of the mustard seed. Both parables demonstrate that the kingdom of heaven has begun on earth in a humble manner, as small as a tiny mustard seed, but that it expands and grows just as leaven expands dough, and a tiny mustard seed grows into a large mustard tree.

The image of a pinch of yeast permeating or influencing fifty pounds of dough parallels the great impact the kingdom of God will have upon all the earth, despite its small beginnings. As yeast influences a batch of dough, so the kingdom of heaven spreads through a person's life. The kingdom of heaven is indeed active, though not fully visible to the world, because it begins with an inner transformation of the heart.

Although yeast looks like a minor ingredient, it permeates the whole loaf of bread. In the same way, although the kingdom of heaven begins very small and is nearly invisible, it will continue to grow and have a great impact on the entire world. As yeast permeates a batch of dough, so the kingdom of heaven spreads through a person's life. God's people are crucial to the advancement of the kingdom of heaven here on earth. As the kingdom of heaven breaks forth, God's people are to break forth with it in unity, with one mind and heart.

The kingdom of God does not consist in words but in power (1 Corinthians 4:20). The kingdom of God will influence the hearts of men and women and expand to the nations of the world, just as yeast expands dough.

God's children should be like yeast that is anointed by God to influence the world with the Spirit of God and to bring down the glory and power of the kingdom of heaven to the earth. The children of God are called to influence the whole world like yeast influences the whole loaf of bread. We are called to enlighten the nations with the power of the gospel of the kingdom of heaven. As the kingdom of God expands here on earth like yeast expands a batch of dough, we are to expand in our love, peace, mercy, and proclamation of the good news of the kingdom.

Chapter 6

The Parable of the Growing Seed

The kingdom of God is like this," He said. "A man scatters seed on the ground; he sleeps and rises—night and day, and the seed sprouts and grows—he doesn't know how. The soil produces a crop by itself—first the blade, then the head, and then the ripe grain on the head. But as soon as the crop is ready, he sends for the sickle, because the harvest has come. (Mark 4:26-29)

Up to this point, our study has focused mainly on parables found in Matthew's gospel. In this chapter, however, we shall examine a parable found only in the gospel of Mark: the parable of the growing seed. This is one of the shortest, and possibly least examined, of the parables.

Identifying the specific audience that initially heard this parable should help in our interpretation of it. In this case, Jesus was teaching a large crowd that had gathered by a body of water, almost certainly the Sea of Galilee. According to Mark 4:1, "The crowd that gathered around him was so large that he got into a boat and sat in it out on the lake, while all the people

The Parables of the Kingdom

were along the shore at the water's edge" (NIV). This parable was not taught in an intimate setting to a small group of believers but rather to a large number of people who were probably at various stages in their spiritual development.[12]

Jesus does not tell us what each item in this parable represents, but the parable goes along with the other parables in the chapter. Earlier in the chapter, Jesus explained the parable of the sower. In that parable, Jesus identified the seed as the Word of God. We can assume, then, that the seed also represents the Word of God in the parable of the growing seed.

The parable of the growing seed, along with the parables that are before and after it in Mark 4, are all related to the kingdom of God and to one another. To understand the parable of the growing seed, we need to understand first the parable of the sower. And to understand the parable of the mustard seed, we need to understand first the parable of the sower and the parable of the growing seed.

The parable of the growing seed describes how the Word of God produces fruit and how the kingdom of heaven grows. Like seed, God's kingdom contains within itself the power to grow. The only human role is planting. Once planted, seeds grow and produce a harvest.

What does this parable reveal about the kingdom of God? We can discern at least three things:

1. It reveals that the kingdom of heaven grows as the Word of God produces fruit.
2. It shows that the growth produced by the Word, or seed, is a mystery, and thus the growth of the kingdom of heaven here on earth is a mystery.
3. Since the kingdom of God grows by virtue of the

---
12 Curry, *The Parable Discovery*

Word of God being planted, its amazing growth is similar to what we observe in the sowing of grain. This parable, then, reveals that the kingdom of God grows and advances just like a mustard seed. Its growth is gradual. It grows slowly but surely, making or leaving an impact along the way as it grows in the human heart.

In the parable of the growing seed, just as in the parable of the sower and the parable of the mustard seed, the seed represents the Word of God. The growth produced by the Word of God is a mystery (Mark 4:26–28). The sower can sow the seed and see it sprout and grow, but the growth is beyond his comprehension. The growth also is gradual. It does not grow all at once but step by step: first the blade, then the head, then the full grain.

This parable illustrates what the kingdom of heaven is like. It is like a seed that is planted and grows into a full grain. The kingdom of heaven is ever growing and ever increasing. It cannot be stopped or destroyed. From the days of Jesus to today, the kingdom of God has been powerfully breaking forth and advancing in the nations of the world.

Chapter 7

The Parables of the Hidden Treasure and the Priceless Pearl

The Value of the Kingdom of Heaven

How valuable is the kingdom of heaven? Is it worth pursuing? Is it worth giving up everything to acquire it? Is it worth living for? To answer these questions, we turn to the parables of the hidden treasure and the priceless pearl. In these twin parables, we discover the immense value of the kingdom of heaven. In fact, they teach us that the kingdom of heaven is of such great value a wise person should be willing to give up all he has in order to obtain it.

The two parables are brief and to the point.

The kingdom of heaven is like treasure, buried in a field, that a man found and reburied. Then in his joy he goes and sells everything he has and buys that field. Again, the kingdom of heaven is like a merchant in search of fine pearls. When he found one priceless pearl, he went and sold everything he had, and bought it. (Matthew 13:44–46)

Jesus had just explained to His disciples the meaning of the parable of the wheat and the weeds. Now He continued by offering them these two parables that demonstrate the immeasurable value of God's kingdom.

The Context of the Parables

In the Jewish culture of Jesus' day, it was common practice for people departing for battle or going on a long journey to bury their treasures in the ground to keep them from thieves. If they returned safely, they could reclaim their buried treasure; but if not, the location of their hidden treasures would remain a mystery. Because of this, some people in the nation of Israel made their living as treasure hunters. Proverbs 2:3–5 and Job 3:20–21 refer to the pursuit of hidden treasures.

Even though people would hunt for these hidden treasures, the treasures still belonged to the person who owned the property. If the treasure hunter discovered a hidden treasure, he would have to purchase the land to become its legal and rightful owner. Thus we see in Matthew 13:44, that after the man in Jesus' parable had found the treasure in a field, he had to buy that field so that he could be the rightful owner of the land and the treasure in it.

Jesus' main focus in the parable of the hidden treasure was on the value the man who discovered the treasure placed on it. The treasure meant everything to him; so the man sold everything he had in order to obtain it. The man's urgency, desire, and passion to make the treasure his is amazing. He even reburied the treasure, hiding it so that no one else could find it.

The parable of the priceless pearl conveys the same idea. The pearl merchant who finds one perfect and priceless pearl is willing to sell everything he has in order to purchase that one pearl. The kingdom of heaven is the greatest treasure a person can ever find. Its immense value and benefit are more than we can even imagine. It should be sought with passion and urgency. We must be willing to give up everything in order to pursue and obtain it. It is worth our money, it is worth our life, it is worth our time, and it is worth our service.

The rich young ruler who came to Jesus in Matthew 19:16–26 did not value the kingdom of heaven as much as he valued his possessions. When Jesus asked him to sell all his belongings and give them to the poor so that he could have treasure in heaven, the young man went away grieving. The ruler proved by his reaction to Jesus' directive that he did not value eternal life more than he valued his own possessions.

Jesus then said to His disciples in Matthew 19:23 that it is hard for a rich person to enter the kingdom of heaven. It is not that riches are bad; but when a person treasures his riches more than he treasures the kingdom of heaven, his riches are a hindrance to him.

The Teaching of the Parables

The parables of the hidden treasure and the priceless pearl teach us these truths:

- The kingdom of heaven is a priceless treasure that is to be desired above all else and at all cost.
- Acquiring the kingdom of heaven requires that we give up everything that would prevent us from being part of it.

- We must seek with urgency the kingdom of heaven.
- The kingdom of heaven is of immense value.

When a person finds the kingdom of heaven, he finds life, hope, happiness, joy, and a future. The kingdom of heaven has arrived. It has arrived to give us all these blessings and to empower us to do the will of our Father here on earth.

Chapter 8
The Parable of the Net

After the parables of the hidden treasure (Matthew 13:44) and the priceless pearl (verses 45–46), Jesus continued to teach about the kingdom with the parable of the net.

> Again, the kingdom of heaven is like a large net thrown into the sea. It collected every kind of fish, and when it was full, they dragged it ashore, sat down, and gathered the good fish into containers, but threw out the worthless ones. So it will be at the end of the age. The angels will go out, separate the evil people from the righteous, and throw them into the blazing furnace. In that place there will be weeping and gnashing of teeth. (Matthew 13:47–50)

The kingdom of God is like a fishing net. What is pictured here is a large net used by fishermen in Jesus' day and still used today in some parts of the world to catch all kinds of fish. It is weighted on one side with lead and buoyed on the opposite edge by wooden floats or corks. The net often is spread between two fishing boats, enabling cooperating fishermen to capture fish across a wide area.

The central theme of this parable is that in the age to come, Yahweh will separate the citizens of the kingdom of heaven from those who are in Satan's kingdom. All who have rejected Jesus as the King of kings—and thus rejected His kingdom—will spend eternity in the lake of fire (hell).

The parable of the net is another simple illustration that teaches about the kingdom of heaven and what it is like. When fishermen put a net into the water, they expect to catch all kinds of fish, good and bad. Only when they pull the net to the shore do they separate the fish, keeping the good ones and throwing away the bad ones.

Jesus compared the fisherman's net to the kingdom of heaven. Just as the fisherman catches all kinds of fish and later separates the good ones from the bad ones, so it will be at the end of the age. The angels of God will separate the righteous people from the wicked ones; only the righteous will inherit the kingdom of heaven.

The parable of the net closely parallels the parable of the wheat and weeds, and it has the same meaning. It describes the final judgment in which the righteous are separated from those who reject Christ and His rule and thus are thrown into the lake of fire. The kingdom is now, and the judgment is in the future. *Now* is the time to accept and allow God's kingdom to influence us and consume our lives.

Chapter 9

The New and Old Treasures

"Have you understood all these things?" "Yes," they told Him. "Therefore," He said to them, "every student of Scripture instructed in the kingdom of heaven is like a landowner who brings out of his storeroom what is new and what is old." When Jesus had finished these parables, He left there. (Matthew 13:51-53)

Jesus concluded His series of parables in Matthew 13 by telling His disciples, "Every student of Scripture instructed in the kingdom of heaven is like a landowner who brings out of his storeroom what is new and what is old." This statement is important, and we cannot ignore it as students of the Word of God. So let's briefly look at Matthew 13:51–53.

The central theme of these verses is that students of Scripture instructed in the kingdom of heaven must share the good news of the kingdom liberally. Jesus' disciples had unique and constant exposure to Jesus' teaching, as He disclosed what had previously been hidden (Matthew 13:34–35). They were well prepared to teach the truth, for in their storeroom, or treasure, of instruction, they had *old* treasures (the Old Testament) and *new* treasures (the teachings of Jesus).

Matthew 13:51–53 shows that Jesus' desire was for His students (disciples) to instruct people both from the old treasures and from the new ones. The Old Testament points the way to Jesus, the Messiah, who is revealed fully in the New Testament. Both Testaments give practical guidelines for faith and for living a kingdom lifestyle here on earth.

The good news of the kingdom is not confined to just the New Testament or just the Old Testament; rather, it draws upon *both* the New and Old Testaments. The religious leaders of Jesus' day were trapped in the Old and blind to the New (which was being introduced by Jesus' teachings), which is why they rejected Jesus the Messiah. They were looking for a future kingdom preceded by judgment. They were expecting a physical, military kind of Messiah. Jesus, however, taught that the kingdom is now and the judgment is future.

Just as the teachers of religious law in Jesus' day were trapped in the Old Testament and blind to the coming New Testament, many Christians today are trapped in the New Testament and blind to the Old Testament. It is important to understand that the New has its foundation in the Old. The New is an extension of the Old. Of course, not everything in the Old Testament is applicable to us, because Jesus fulfilled the law, but that does not mean we can throw it all away.

The Old Testament is a real treasure; its teaching is rich and powerful and points the way to Jesus, the Messiah. When the teachings of the Old Testament are combined with those of the New, they produce in us a deeper, wider, and higher understanding of the kingdom of God.

The kingdom of heaven is not only to be experienced; it also must be shared and proclaimed. As disciples of Jesus Christ, we must desire not only to learn about the mystery and power of the kingdom of heaven but also to teach and instruct our family and friends and all the nations in the ways of God, drawing from our storeroom of new and old teachings so that people can understand God on a deeper level.

Chapter 10

The Parable of the Unforgiving Servant

Then Peter came to Him and said, "Lord, how many times could my brother sin against me and I forgive him? As many as seven times?"

"I tell you, not as many as seven," Jesus said to him, "but 70 times seven. For this reason, the kingdom of heaven can be compared to a king who wanted to settle accounts with his slaves. When he began to settle accounts, one who owed 10,000 talents was brought before him. Since he had no way to pay it back, his master commanded that he, his wife, his children, and everything he had be sold to pay the debt.

At this, the slave fell facedown before him and said, 'Be patient with me, and I will pay you everything!' Then the master of that slave had compassion, released him, and forgave him the loan.

But that slave went out and found one of his fellow

The Parables of the Kingdom

slaves who owed him 100 denarii. He grabbed him, started choking him, and said, 'Pay what you owe!'

At this, his fellow slave fell down and began begging him, 'Be patient with me, and I will pay you back.' But he wasn't willing. On the contrary, he went and threw him into prison until he could pay what was owed. When the other slaves saw what had taken place, they were deeply distressed and went and reported to their master everything that had happened.

Then, after he had summoned him, his master said to him, 'You wicked slave! I forgave you all that debt because you begged me. Shouldn't you also have had mercy on your fellow slave, as I had mercy on you?' And his master got angry and handed him over to the jailers to be tortured until he could pay everything that was owed. So My heavenly Father will also do to you if each of you does not forgive his brother from his heart." (Matthew 18:21–35)

Jesus continued to teach His disciples the principles that govern the kingdom of heaven. In this passage He used one of the most profound and practical stories ever told to demonstrate the mercies of Yahweh. Peter came to Jesus and asked Him, "How often will my brother sin against me, and I forgive him? As many as seven times?" Jesus responded to Peter's question by saying, "I do not say to you seven times, but seventy times seven" (ESV).

Within Judaism, forgiving a person three times was considered sufficient to show a forgiving spirit. In fact, some rabbis required that their students forgive an offender *only* three times. This was based on the following Scriptures:

> God certainly does all these things two or three times to a man in order to turn him back from the Pit, so he may shine with the light of life. (Job 33:29–30)

> The LORD says: I will not relent from punishing Damascus for three crimes, even four, because they threshed Gilead with iron sledges. (Amos 1:3)

> The LORD says: I will not relent from punishing Israel for three crimes, even four, because they sell a righteous person for silver and a needy person for a pair of sandals (Amos 2:6)

Peter probably considered his suggestion of forgiving someone seven times very gracious in comparison to three times. But in Matthew 18:22 Jesus went far beyond even this by saying that one is to forgive his offender seventy times seven.

There is debate among Bible interpreters as to whether the language used here means Jesus was demanding forgiveness of an offending brother 77 times or 490 times (70 times 7). Whichever it is, the point Jesus was making is that in the kingdom of heaven forgiveness is unlimited when true repentance is present. Forgiving without keeping count of how many times someone has wronged you is true kingdom forgiveness. The disciples of Jesus are to forgive without keeping count (seventy times seven).

A Kingdom of Mercy

The king in Jesus' parable forgave his servant's huge debt. But suddenly the focus of the story shifts from the compassionate heart of the king to the stony and unmerciful heart of the forgiven servant. The forgiven servant saw his fellow servant and confronted him aggressively about his debt. He quickly forgot that the king had just forgiven him his own massive debt.

An opportunity to extend the mercy the servant had just received from the king to his fellow servant presented itself, but he failed to forgive his colleague. In him there was no mercy, no compassion, and no forgiveness. The king's mercy and forgiveness of his debt meant nothing to him.

As we can see in the story, the unforgiving servant owed the king far more money than his fellow servant owed him. The forgiveness of the king should have motivated him to forgive his colleague, but he did not. The king was infuriated by the attitude of the unforgiving servant. He called him a "wicked servant" and handed him over to the jailers to be tortured until he paid back all that he owed the king.

The word translated "jailers" literally means "torturers." The debtor's torture would continue until the debt was paid in full.

The Meaning of the Parable

In this parable, the king symbolizes God, and the settling of accounts symbolizes divine judgment. The king's forgiveness of such a massive debt is a dramatic illustration of God's forgiveness of our many sins. Our sins call for God's judgment, but because of His mercy, God has forgiven our sins through the death and resurrection of His Son, Jesus Christ.

In biblical times, serious consequences awaited those who could not pay their debts. A lender could seize the borrower who could not repay the loan and force him or his family to work until the debt was paid. The debtor also could be thrown into prison, or his family could be sold into slavery to help pay off the debt. Similarly, before we accepted Christ's death in payment for our sins, death was waiting for us, because we had no power or ability to pay our debt of sin.

The unpayable debt in Jesus' parable illustrates the enormity of our sins, which carry a debt far greater than we could ever hope to pay. The forgiveness of the king represents not only God's forgiveness of us, freeing us from the power of sin and death, but also His justification of us—putting us in right standing with Him through His Son, Jesus Christ. In return, we are obligated to exercise forgiveness and mercy to others.

In Matthew 18:32–35, Jesus revealed the point He was making in this parable. Since the king (God) had shown the servant such great mercy by forgiving his debt, he should have forgiven the debt of his fellow servant. Because God has forgiven believers of all their sins, they should not withhold forgiveness from others. The realization of how completely Christ has forgiven us should produce in us an attitude of forgiveness toward others.

Forgiveness in the Kingdom of God

Not only did Jesus teach the importance and necessity of forgiveness, but He also demonstrated the willingness to forgive at an even higher level. Scripture shows us how Jesus illustrated the kingdom of God through forgiveness. In Matthew 9:2–8, He forgave the paralyzed man's sins. In John 8:3–11, He forgave the woman who was caught in adultery. In Luke 7:44–50,

The Parables of the Kingdom

He forgave the sins of a woman who anointed his feet with perfume. In Luke 23:39–43 we see Jesus forgiving the criminal on the cross. And Luke 23:34 records that Jesus even forgave the people who crucified Him.

The parable of the unforgiving servant demonstrates the character of God. God is merciful and forgiving. His kingdom is full of mercy and forgiveness. The king in the parable is a perfect picture of God. He was moved with compassion toward his servant and forgave his debt. In the same way, God was moved with compassion and mercy toward sinful mankind, and He sacrificed His only Son, Jesus Christ, as payment for our debt (Romans 5:8–11; John 3:16).

In God's eyes, the hallmark of a Christian is forgiving those who offend us without keeping a record of their wrongs. This can be a very difficult thing to do. However, the key is simply to remember that God has forgiven us; therefore, we also can—and should—forgive others.

Through this parable we learn that God is forgiving, but we also learn that He judges those who refuse to forgive others. Forgiveness means pardoning the unpardonable; anything less is not forgiveness at all. Forgiveness also means erasing all wrongs done against us. As disciples of Jesus Christ, we must not keep a record or count the wrongs done to us; rather, we must demonstrate to others the same spirit of forgiveness we have freely received from God.

Effective Forgiveness

If your brother sins against you, go and rebuke him in private. If he listens to you, you have won your brother. But if he won't listen, take one or two more with you, so that by the testimony of two or three witnesses every fact may be established. If he pays no attention to them, tell the church. But if he doesn't pay attention even to the church, let him be like an unbeliever and a tax collector to you. (Matthew 18:15–17)

In these verses just prior to Jesus' parable, Jesus clearly taught His disciples the importance of dealing directly with offenses in order to restore a brother who has sinned. Nowhere in these verses do we see Jesus teaching us to ignore, avoid, or forget the issue at hand. Many people think forgiveness is simply forgetting the wrong somebody has done. That is not forgiveness. Indeed, forgetting the wrong done to us is *part* of forgiveness, but it is not in itself forgiveness. Effective forgiveness takes place when people humble themselves and sit down to iron out their differences.

Effective forgiveness does not just let something slip by but instead deals with the matter at hand. Avoiding or ignoring the wrong somebody has done causes more damage to a relationship and creates more problems. In fact, ignoring or avoiding the matter builds up hatred, anger, and bitterness and feeds the spirit of unforgiveness.

If somebody sins against us or strays from Christ, we must follow the process outlined in Matthew 18:15 in order to effectively restore our relationship with the person and help restore that person's relationship with God. Many Christians—as well as non-Christians—struggle with unforgiveness simply because they choose to ignore or avoid sin issues rather than deal with the offender face to face.

When someone wrongs us, we often do the opposite of what Jesus commands here. We turn away in hatred or resentment, seek revenge, or engage in gossip. Jesus said we should go to that person first, as difficult as that may be, and we should forgive that person as often as he or she needs it (Matthew 18:21–22). Following the biblical procedure will definitely create a much better chance of restoring the relationship.

Forgiveness is a crucial element in the kingdom of heaven because it causes God's children to move forward in the Lord and not backward. Lack of forgiveness moves the church, the body of Christ, backward—it stops the advancement of the kingdom of heaven here on earth. *To receive forgiveness from God and refuse to forgive others is sin in God's eyes.*

Chapter 11

The Parable of the Lost Sheep

In the parable of the unforgiving servant, Jesus demonstrated the forgiving and compassionate heart of God the Father. That same theme is presented in Luke 15, where Jesus shared three other parables that illustrate the forgiving heart of God. These parables are the parable of the lost sheep, the parable of the lost coin, and the parable of the prodigal son. In all these parables, God is pictured as a God of compassion, mercy, forgiveness, and restoration.

The first of these, the parable of the lost sheep, is found in Luke 15:1–7:

> All the tax collectors and sinners were approaching to listen to Him. And the Pharisees and scribes were complaining, "This man welcomes sinners and eats with them!"
>
> So He told them this parable: "What man among you, who has 100 sheep and loses one of them, does not leave the 99 in the open field and go after the lost one until

The Parables of the Kingdom

he finds it? When he has found it, he joyfully puts it on his shoulders, and coming home, he calls his friends and neighbors together, saying to them, 'Rejoice with me, because I have found my lost sheep!' I tell you, in the same way, there will be more joy in heaven over one sinner who repents than over 99 righteous people who don't need repentance."

This parable also is recorded in Matthew 18:12–14.

The tax collectors and sinners came to listen to Jesus, but Israel's religious leaders complained about their presence. They grumbled that Jesus welcomed sinners and tax collectors and ate with them. In response to the complaints of the Pharisees and scribes, Jesus told the parable of the lost sheep, basically to demonstrate that the kingdom of heaven is all about mercy, forgiveness, and restoration.

The religious leaders in Jesus' day were careful to stay "clean," according to the Old Testament law. However, they went even beyond the law in their avoidance of certain sinners and those who had leprosy. According to the Gospels, Jesus did the opposite: He touched those who had leprosy and ate with sinners and with tax collectors, who were the most despised people in the community and considered among the worst of sinners.

In the parable of the lost sheep, Jesus emphasized how much God cares for every lost sinner and how joyfully He responds when one repents. He demonstrated God's loving concern for sinners with the natural concern one has for even one lost sheep out of a hundred. Jesus asked His listeners, "What man among you, who has 100 sheep and loses one of them, does not leave the 99 in the open field and go after the lost one until he finds it?" (verse 4). In the Palestine of that day, every sheep was valuable and worthy of the effort put forth to find it when it went astray. Likewise, God pursues sinners and rejoices when one is saved.

Chapter 12

The Parable of the Lost Coin

To elaborate further on the importance of lost sinners in the eyes of God, Jesus told another parable, the parable of the lost coin, in Luke 15:8–10.

> "Or what woman who has 10 silver coins, if she loses one coin, does not light a lamp, sweep the house, and search carefully until she finds it? When she finds it, she calls her women friends and neighbors together, saying, 'Rejoice with me, because I have found the silver coin I lost!' I tell you, in the same way, there is joy in the presence of God's angels over one sinner who repents."

Luke 15:1–2 gives us the context in which Jesus taught this parable: "All the tax collectors and sinners were approaching to listen to Him. And the Pharisees and scribes were complaining, 'This man welcomes sinners and eats with them!'" Welcoming people and sharing a meal with them typically indicates acceptance of them. As far as the Pharisees and the teachers of the law (scribes) were concerned, it was not acceptable for someone like Jesus to welcome and eat with people considered in the community to be sinners.

The Pharisees and scribes considered themselves righteous and all others wicked. Jesus addressed their prideful attitude with the parables of the lost sheep, the lost coin, and the lost son.

In the second parable, Jesus taught that just as a woman would rejoice at finding her lost coin, so the angels rejoice over a sinner who repents. Each individual is precious and important to God. God grieves over every loss and rejoices whenever a lost sinner is "found" and brought into His kingdom. The parable of the lost coin, like the parable of the lost sheep, focuses on the joy of restoration and on sharing that joyful experience with friends and neighbors. The main message in these two parables is that we should rejoice with God when that which was lost has been found.

God is a great and merciful God. When lost individuals (sinners) repent of their sins, He welcomes them into His kingdom with great rejoicing. In Matthew 9:12 Jesus said, "Those who are well don't need a doctor, but the sick do." This is why He welcomed sinners into His presence. They had a need that only the Great Physician could meet. Sadly, because of their observance of the law, the self-righteous Pharisees and scribes considered themselves healthy before God and without need of repentance, even though they were spiritually sick and blind.

Christians are able to understand a God who forgives sinners who turn to Him for mercy. However, a God who tenderly searches for sinners and then joyfully forgives them must possess an extraordinary love. This is the kind of love that prompted God to send Yeshua to earth. He is the Great Shepherd sent from heaven to search for and rescue us, the lost sheep.

In the parables of the lost sheep and the lost coin, as well

The Parables of the Kingdom

as in the parable that follows (the parable of the lost son), Jesus painted a great picture of God's grace in His desire to see the lost saved. God cares for the lost, and He values them. His kingdom has arrived for all sinners who repent and turn to Him.

Chapter 13

The Parable of the Lost (Prodigal) Son

To expand further on God's care, compassion, love, and mercy for the lost, Jesus told another parable in Luke 15:11–32, the parable of the prodigal son.

> He also said: "A man had two sons. The younger of them said to his father, 'Father, give me the share of the estate I have coming to me.' So he distributed the assets to them. Not many days later, the younger son gathered together all he had and traveled to a distant country, where he squandered his estate in foolish living. After he had spent everything, a severe famine struck that country, and he had nothing. Then he went to work for one of the citizens of that country, who sent him into his fields to feed pigs. He longed to eat his fill from the carob pods the pigs were eating, but no one would give him any. When he came to his senses, he said, 'How many of my father's hired hands have more than enough food, and here I am dying of hunger! I'll get up, go to my father, and say to him, Father, I have sinned against

heaven and in your sight. I'm no longer worthy to be called your son. Make me like one of your hired hands.' So he got up and went to his father. But while the son was still a long way off, his father saw him and was filled with compassion. He ran, threw his arms around his neck, and kissed him. The son said to him, 'Father, I have sinned against heaven and in your sight. I'm no longer worthy to be called your son.'

"But the father told his slaves, 'Quick! Bring out the best robe and put it on him; put a ring on his finger and sandals on his feet. Then bring the fattened calf and slaughter it, and let's celebrate with a feast, because this son of mine was dead and is alive again; he was lost and is found!' So they began to celebrate.

"Now his older son was in the field; as he came near the house, he heard music and dancing. So he summoned one of the servants and asked what these things meant. 'Your brother is here,' he told him, 'and your father has slaughtered the fattened calf because he has him back safe and sound.'

"Then he became angry and didn't want to go in. So his father came out and pleaded with him. But he replied to his father, 'Look, I have been slaving many years for you, and I have never disobeyed your orders, yet you never gave me a young goat so I could celebrate with my friends. But when this son of yours came, who has devoured your assets with prostitutes, you slaughtered the fattened calf for him.'

"'Son,' he said to him, 'you are always with me, and everything I have is yours. But we had to celebrate and rejoice, because this brother of yours was dead and is alive again; he was lost and is found.'"

Most Bible scholars have concluded that the emphasis of this parable is not simply on the return of the prodigal son but rather on the entire situation. People often tend to focus solely on the return of the prodigal son; yet there are three important players in this parable, and each one of them is important to understanding the meaning and purpose of the parable.

In this parable, Jesus wanted to drive home a very important point, and that point is the compassion of the father for his runaway son. The unforgettable scene of the father forgiving his wayward son overshadows all other concerns. But no one can fully understand the forgiving heart and compassion of the father in this parable without looking at the entire picture, for although the prodigal son is lost, so also is his older brother.

From what we can tell in the parable of the prodigal son, Jesus was trying to show his listeners three things:

1. The lost, but returning son (restoration of a sinner)
2. The older brother's response to the return of his sinful younger brother
3. The compassion and forgiving heart of the father

Context of the Parable

Jesus was still responding to the murmuring by the Pharisees and scribes about His associations with the tax collectors and sinners (Luke 15:1–2). The parable of the prodigal son again illustrated the compassionate heart of God toward the lost.

While it was unusual in Jewish culture for a son to ask for his inheritance while his father was still alive, it was not unheard of. In asking for his inheritance while his father was still alive was actually wishing death to his father. Thus, the younger son's attitude was dishonoring toward his father and would have brought shame to the family.

Inheritance Laws in Ancient Israel

Family inheritance laws in ancient Israel were designed to favor the firstborn son by giving him a double share, probably with the purpose of keeping a family's name, land, and holdings together and intact (Numbers 27:8–11; 36:7–9; Deuteronomy 21:17). The oldest son would receive two shares of his father's inheritance, while each of the other sons received one share.

In Jewish culture, the older son would be the executor, or administrator, of his father's possessions and assume the role as family head after his father's death. Sometimes an older son would decide not to split up the family holdings among the brothers (see Luke 12:13). If the father had no sons to inherit his possessions (land), they would then be passed on to his daughters and then down the family line.

Dividing up a father's estate before his death was known practice in the Jewish community but only if the father himself decided to do so. In this case, the property would pass to the sons—again with the oldest receiving a double portion—but the father would have the right to enjoy the profits of the properties until his death.

The Teaching of the Parable

In this parable, the younger son is a picture of lost people such as the tax collectors and sinners of that day, while the elder brother is a perfect picture of the Pharisees and teachers of the law. This is why many Bible scholars have concluded that both these brothers picture the lost. In fact, the parable is sometimes referred to as the parable of the two lost sons.

It is very, very important to understand that the parable of the prodigal son focuses on the crisis of a broken relationship between a human being and God (son and father). A person living without God is like the prodigal son who runs away to a far country. Yet his brother living at home with his father is no better off. He is much like a religious person who misunderstands the divine nature and lacks a meaningful relationship with the heavenly Father.

In every scene of the parable, the father plays the role of the compassionate parent. He loves his sons, and he is ready and willing to forgive them when they make mistakes. He seeks restoration and healing of relationships, but neither of the sons understands him as a loving and compassionate parent.

After he has squandered all the inheritance given to him by his father and his living conditions are rapidly deteriorating, the younger son begins to reflect on his condition and realizes that even his father's servants have it better than he does. His painful and harsh conditions help him to see his father in a new light and bring him hope. He makes the right move and decides to return to his father.

While the son is still a long way off, his father sees him returning and is filled with compassion (the key to this parable). He runs to him, throws his arms around his neck, and kisses him. The son does something special too: he humbles himself and says to his father, "I have sinned against heaven and before you. I am no longer worthy to be called your son." The father responds by telling his servants to quickly bring out

The Parables of the Kingdom

the best robe and put it on his son and to put a ring on his finger and sandals on his feet. He does not stop there; he commands his servants to bring the fattened calf and slaughter it for the celebration. The lost son has been found, and this calls for rejoicing.

This is the point at which the parable ties in to the two previous parables of the lost sheep and the lost coin. In all these parables, Jesus clearly pictured some of the attributes of God. God rejoices in saving the lost, and His heart is open to receive repentant sinners. This stands in contrast to the contempt the Pharisees and scribes displayed for the tax collectors and sinners who came to Jesus (Luke 15:2).

The story then takes a sudden twist, and the focus shifts from the repentant and returning son to the older brother. The older brother is boiling hot with anger, offended and jealous over the father's celebration for his younger brother. He is angry at his father's forgiving love; he would rather see his father punish his younger brother than celebrate his return, especially since the younger man had squandered his inheritance.

The older brother depicts the religious leaders of Jesus' day. They worked very hard at keeping the law, and in their self-righteousness they were angered that sinners were coming to Jesus. Surely, they thought, if Jesus were a righteous king, He would not welcome these sinners into His presence. However, Jesus is a different kind of king with a different kind of kingdom. He has come down from heaven to seek and to save sinners.

The parable of the prodigal son powerfully teaches us about God's true nature and character. The father in the parable represents God. His younger son, in the opinion of many Christian scholars, represents a runaway Christian, or a backslider. His older son, then, would represent a Christian who is still in his father's house (God's house) but who lacks forgiveness in his heart for his returning and sinful younger brother.

As much as He is a God of judgment, God also is a compassionate Father, full of mercy, love, grace, and forgiveness. His love for the lost is indescribable and beyond human understanding. The parables of the lost sheep, the lost coin, and the prodigal son all picture lost sinners being found by Jesus and the rejoicing that results from it.

Chapter 14

The Parable of the Day Laborers (Vineyard)

For the kingdom of heaven is like the master of a household, who went out early in the morning to hire workers for his vineyard. And he went out about the third hour and saw others standing in the marketplace, idle. And to them he said, you go into the vineyard too, and I'll give you whatever is right. So they went. Again he went out about the sixth and ninth hour and did the same.

And about the eleventh hour, he went out and found others standing around. And he said to them, 'Why have you been standing here idle the whole day?' 'Because no one hired us,' they said to him. He said to them, 'You go into the vineyard, too.' Now when evening came, the owner of the vineyard said to his foreman, 'Call the workers and pay them their wages, beginning from the last to the first.' And those who had come about the eleventh hour each received a denarius. And when the first came, they supposed that they would receive more; yet they too received a denarius.

But when they received it, they began to grumble against the master of the house, saying, 'These last guys did one hour, and you've made them equal to us, who bore the burden and scorching heat of the day!' But answering, he said to one of them, 'Friend, I am doing you no wrong. Didn't you agree with me on a denarius? Take what is yours and go. But I want to give this last guy the same as you. Am I not permitted to do what I want with what belongs to me? Or is your eye evil because I am good?' So the last will be first, and the first last. (Matthew 20:1–16 Tree of Life Bible)

Jesus employed a lot of Jewish illustrations (some of them humorous) to make His listeners redefine their view of God's character and nature. In this parable, Jesus again showed that the character and nature of God is beyond human understanding. The landowner's decision to pay all the workers the same amount was astonishing to the people of Jesus' day, as it would be for people with a twenty-first century mind-set.

We must remember the Jewish religious environment in which Jesus was teaching. The religious leaders of the day considered themselves more righteous than anyone else, because they strictly observed the law of God. In Jesus' eyes, however, these self-righteous people were far from God, and God would treat them as being no different from others.

The religious leaders, who had kept the law of God all their lives, would not receive a higher reward than those (Gentiles) who had just started following the Lord. All would receive the same reward. Jesus' parable of the day laborers illustrated this principle.

The landowner in the parable is a picture of God, and all

The Parables of the Kingdom

the workers hired stand for God's true people, those who labor in His kingdom. The landowner recruits workers to work in his vineyard, hiring workers at various times of the day. The people hired expect Him to pay them differently, even after they have all agreed on the wage. They think the ones who started working earlier should get more than the ones who started at nine and that the ones who started at nine should be paid more than those who started work between noon and three. And the ones who started between noon and three should be paid more than the ones who just started working at five. In other words, those who started at five should get less than everyone else. After all, they worked only a few hours and so should be paid less, while the ones who had started work earlier should be paid more. However, the landowner (God) does not think that way. He is a different kind of "boss" or "manager" with a different heart, character, and nature. He pays all the workers the same, starting with the ones he hired at five. All are paid the same amount: one denarius.

The question that must be asked is why he pays them all the same amount, despite the unequal duration of their work. The last workers to be hired did not deserve the same payment as the first workers to be hired, but because of the master's generosity, they are paid the same wage. The landowner (God) extends His graciousness and generosity to the latecomers.

In the kingdom of heaven, some appear deserving of a higher reward than others, but God rewards all according to His grace and mercy. All true disciples of Jesus, whether Jews or Gentiles, are equal in His eyes.

Through the parable of the day laborers (or parable of the vineyard), Jesus revealed the character and nature of God and the nature of His kingdom. The main focus is on the generous and gracious nature of God. He does things as He pleases and not as people wish or please. His grace is given to all in equal measure because He is no respecter of persons (Acts 10:34–35). God is fair, and He is just; but no one can comprehend His immeasurable goodness and His unmerited generosity.

This parable teaches us about the unmerited grace of God, which is beyond human understanding. A criminal who repents just before his death is forgiven and invited to be with Jesus in paradise (Luke 23:40–43). Yet many people resent God's gracious acceptance of the despised, the outcasts, and the sinners who turn to Him for forgiveness.

God extends His forgiveness, grace, and mercy to all who repent and desire to turn their lives around. As demonstrated by Jesus in this parable, as in the parable of the prodigal son, the kingdom of heaven is full of grace. God's generosity is more abundant than anyone would expect or imagine. God is indeed a merciful God; yet He is also a God of judgment, and it is important to understand that God's grace and mercy is not a passport for people to do any evil they desire.

In all the parables of the kingdom we have covered so far, we have seen that Jesus taught the principles that govern the kingdom of heaven. Through the parables, He revealed to His disciples the character and nature of God. He shared with them how the kingdom of heaven grows and advances here on earth and how God is a merciful, loving, and forgiving Father.

As followers of Jesus, we are to emulate God's character and nature and demonstrate His qualities in our lives as we go out to proclaim the arrival of the kingdom of heaven here on earth. God is a forgiving Father, and we who have experienced love and forgiveness from Him must in return love and forgive others unconditionally. God has called us to be ambassadors of love and not hate, peace and not destruction, life and not death.

Chapter 15

The Parable of the Two Sons

But what do you think? A man had two sons. He went to the first and said, 'My son, go, work in the vineyard today.'

He answered, 'I don't want to!' Yet later he changed his mind and went. Then the man went to the other and said the same thing.

'I will, sir,' he answered. But he didn't go.

Which of the two did his father's will?"

The first," they said.

Jesus said to them, "I assure you: Tax collectors and prostitutes are entering the kingdom of God before you! For John came to you in the way of righteousness, and you didn't believe him. Tax collectors and prostitutes did believe him, but you, when you saw it, didn't even change your minds then and believe him. (Matthew 21:28–32)

The key interpretive point in understanding the parable of the two sons comes from defining the audience to whom Jesus was speaking. For that, we must look at the overall context of this passage. Matthew 21 begins with Jesus' triumphal entry into Jerusalem. The crowd responded by shouting, "Hosanna to the Son of David! He who comes in the name of the Lord is the blessed one! Hosanna in the highest heaven!" (Matthew 21:9).

"The whole city was shaken, saying, 'Who is this?' And the crowds kept saying, 'This is the prophet Jesus from Nazareth in Galilee!'" (Matthew 21:10–11). The first thing Jesus did in the city was cleanse the temple complex (verses 12–13). The next day Jesus was teaching in the temple, when the chief priests and the elders of the people came to him and challenged his authority:

> By what authority are you doing these things? Who gave you this authority?" Jesus answered them, "I will also ask you one question, and if you answer it for Me, then I will tell you by what authority I do these things. Where did John's baptism come from? From heaven or from men?" . . . They answered Jesus, "We don't know." And He said to them, "Neither will I tell you by what authority I do these things." (Matthew 21:23–24, 27).

Jesus then told them the parable of the two sons.

The audience to whom Jesus was speaking was made up primarily of the Pharisees and Jewish leaders of the day. The parable of the two sons demonstrates these religious leaders' failure to respond appropriately to John the Baptist's message. They were hypocrites who did not live up to their talk. They acted like the second son in the parable, who said yes to his father but did not go to work in his father's vineyard. However, the tax collectors and the prostitutes responded well to John the Baptist's message and believed him. They acted like the first son in the parable, who said no at the beginning but later changed his mind and went to work in his father's vineyard.

The father in this parable again represents God, the first son is a picture of sinners such as tax collectors and prostitutes, and the second son represents the chief priests and elders, who promised obedience to God but never fulfilled their commitment. Tax collectors and prostitutes changed their ways upon hearing the preaching of John the Baptist, while the religious leaders did not believe him or change their ways.

The point Jesus was making in this parable is that a person's actions ultimately prove whether that person really follows God. The son who said he would obey but did not, represented many Jewish people of Jesus' day, particularly the religious leaders. They said they would do the will of God, but they constantly disobeyed Him. This parable teaches that what gets people into the kingdom of heaven is not their religious talk or words of commitment but rather their obedience to Jesus and the Word of God.

It is easy for people to say they will do something, but it can be very difficult to put that verbal commitment into action. Many of God's children promise to follow Him with all their hearts but fail to live up to those promises. Thank God for the Holy Spirit. The Holy Spirit is there to help God's people live for the kingdom of heaven. Through the power of the Holy Spirit, God's people can fulfill their commitment to do the will of God.

Chapter 16

The Parable of the Wedding Banquet

Once more Jesus spoke to them in parables: "The kingdom of heaven may be compared to a king who gave a wedding banquet for his son. He sent out his slaves to summon those invited to the banquet, but they didn't want to come. Again, he sent out other slaves, and said, 'Tell those who are invited: Look, I've prepared my dinner; my oxen and fattened cattle have been slaughtered, and everything is ready. Come to the wedding banquet.'

But they paid no attention and went away, one to his own farm, another to his business. And the others seized his slaves, treated them outrageously and killed them. The king was enraged, so he sent out his troops, destroyed those murderers, and burned down their city.

Then he told his slaves, 'The banquet is ready, but those who were invited were not worthy. Therefore go to where the roads exit the city and invite everyone you find to the banquet.' So those slaves went out on the roads and gathered everyone they found, both evil and good. The wedding banquet was filled with guests. But when the king came in to view the guests, he saw a man there who was not dressed for a wedding. So he said to him, 'Friend, how did you get in here without wedding clothes?' The man was speechless.

Then the king told the attendants, 'Tie him up hand and foot, and throw him into the outer darkness, where there will be weeping and gnashing of teeth.'

For many are invited, but few are chosen. (Matthew 22:1–14)

Context of the Parable

The wedding banquet was one of the most joyous festivals of Jewish culture. The celebration could last for weeks. Two invitations were issued when banquets were given. The first asked the guests to attend—much like a modern-day "save the date" card. The second announced that all was ready for the banquet to begin. In this story, the king sent the invitation to his guests three times, and each time they rejected his invitation.

Many people had been invited, but when the time for the banquet came and the table was set, those invited refused to come (verses 4–5). The king's servants, who went out to escort these guests to the banquet, were mistreated and even killed (verse 6). Enraged at the response of those who had been invited, the king sent his army to avenge the deaths of his servants (verse 7). To refuse a direct invitation from the king would be an extreme insult and a dangerous thing to do to someone who possessed such authority and power in the community.

The king in this parable represents God, the son who is being honored at this banquet represents Jesus, and the slaves sent out to invite the guests—and are mistreated and even killed—represent the prophets of Israel. Many prophets, including John the Baptist, in fact had been murdered (Matthew 14:10; 23:37).

The wedding banquet symbolizes the great messianic feast the Jewish people expected to share with the Messiah at the beginning of His rule. The guests, both good and evil, probably represent people of all nations, both Jews and Gentiles, who are invited into the kingdom despite their unworthiness. However, first they must accept the invitation (Jesus Christ). Coming to the feast represents entering the kingdom, and the improperly dressed guest represents a false disciple.

Wedding Garments

While everyone was invited to the banquet, proper wedding garments were still expected. In ancient Israel, it was customary for wedding guests to be given wedding clothes to wear to the banquet. And in Ezekiel 16:10–13, we read of God symbolically clothing His unworthy people in beautiful garments. By not accepting and wearing the garment provided, the one guest greatly insulted the host.

The wedding garments picture the righteousness needed to enter God's kingdom. Christ has provided these garments through the finished work of the cross, but each person must choose to put them on in order to enter the king's banquet hall and inherit eternal life. Christ alone has provided the garments of salvation.

Isaiah 61:10 says, "I greatly rejoice in the LORD, I exult in my God; for He has clothed me with the garments of salvation and wrapped me in a robe of righteousness, as a groom wears a turban and as a bride adorns herself with her jewels."

Many Are Invited, but Few Are Chosen

Many have been invited to the wedding feast, or into the kingdom of God, but not all who are invited will actually accept the invitation, or be "chosen." The word *many* here is inclusive and not restrictive. Everyone is invited to enter the wonderful kingdom of God, but it is up to each individual to accept that invitation.

This parable does not mean that God calls a lot of people, picks over them, and keeps only a few. If that were true, the middle of the parable would have no meaning. Rather, it means that God calls everyone and gives each person the power to respond; but to be chosen, we must respond to the call. The main point here is that the people who were originally invited to the wedding banquet rejected the invitation, and therefore others were invited in their place.

Through this parable, Jesus demonstrated God's invitation to all human beings to join in fellowship with Him in His kingdom. To summarize the point of the parable of the wedding feast; God sent His Son into the world, and the very people who should have celebrated His coming rejected Him. As a result, the kingdom of heaven was opened to anyone willing to accept the Lord Jesus Christ as Lord and Savior.

If the "worthy" had accepted the invitation, the "unworthy" would not have been invited. A dominant theme in Matthew's gospel is the inclusion of the Gentiles among the people of God because of Israel's rejection of Jesus as the Messiah. This is highlighted by the words, "Therefore I tell you, the kingdom of God will be taken away from you and given to a nation producing its fruit" (Matthew 21:43). This is the message emphasized in this parable.

Chapter 17

The Parables of the Ten Virgins and the Talents

The Parable of the Ten Virgins

Then the kingdom of heaven will be like 10 virgins who took their lamps and went out to meet the groom. Five of them were foolish and five were sensible. When the foolish took their lamps, they didn't take olive oil with them. But the sensible ones took oil in their flasks with their lamps. Since the groom was delayed, they all became drowsy and fell asleep.

In the middle of the night there was a shout: 'Here's the groom! Come out to meet him.'

Then all those virgins got up and trimmed their lamps. But the foolish ones said to the sensible ones, 'Give us some of your oil, because our lamps are going out.'

The sensible ones answered, 'No, there won't be enough

for us and for you. Go instead to those who sell, and buy oil for yourselves.'

When they had gone to buy some, the groom arrived. Then those who were ready went in with him to the wedding banquet, and the door was shut.

Later the rest of the virgins also came and said, 'Master, master, open up for us!'

But he replied, 'I assure you: I do not know you!'

Therefore be alert, because you don't know either the day or the hour. (Matthew 25:1–13)

 To clearly understand the context and emphasis of the parable of the ten virgins, we need to begin our study in chapter 24 of Matthew. In Matthew 24 we see Jesus teaching about His second coming; the things that must happen before His coming; and the importance of being ready, or prepared, for His return. As Jesus sat on the Mount of Olives, the place where Zechariah the prophet had prophesied the Messiah would stand when He comes to establish His kingdom (Zechariah 14:4), His disciples privately asked Him, "What is the sign of Your coming and of the end of the age?" (Matthew 24:3).
 Jesus responded by telling His disciples not to be misled. He warned that many would come in His name, claiming to be the Messiah, and they will deceive many. There would be wars and threats of wars, but His followers should not panic because the end wouldn't follow immediately. He said that in those days nations would go to war against each other, and

The Parables of the Kingdom

there would be famines and earthquakes in many parts of the world. All this, however, was just the first of the birth pains, with more to come. Jesus said His disciples would be arrested, persecuted, killed, and hated all over the world because they were Jesus' followers. Many people would turn away from Jesus and betray and hate each other. False prophets would appear and would deceive many people. Sin would become rampant everywhere, and "the love of many will grow cold" (Matthew 24:12). "But," He encouraged them, "the one who endures to the end will be delivered. This good news of the kingdom will be proclaimed in all the world as a testimony to all nations. And then the end will come" (verses 13–14).

In verses 27–31, Jesus gave the disciples the signs that would signal His return: The sun will be darkened, the moon will give no light, the stars will fall from the sky, and the powers in the heaven will be shaken. He will appear in the heavens, and there will be mourning among all the peoples of the earth, as they see Him coming on the clouds of heaven with power and great glory.

However, in Matthew 24:36, Jesus emphasized that no one knows the day or the hour when the end will come—not even the angels in heaven or the Son (Jesus) Himself knows. Only the Father knows.

So, what did all that mean for the disciples? The disciples were to remain faithful and watchful and preach the good news of the kingdom of heaven to all nations. As faithful and sensible servants, the disciples were to take care of God's people by feeding them with the good news of the kingdom, not fighting with other servants or partying or getting drunk as they await the coming of their Master (Matthew 24:45–50). In other words, the disciples were to be prepared because the Master's return would be unannounced and unexpected.

To clarify further and emphasize what it means to be prepared for His return and how to live until He comes back, Jesus told the parable of the ten virgins. Five of the virgins—who appear to be bridesmaids—were ready to meet the bridegroom (Jesus), while the other five were not adequately prepared to meet the bridegroom after He had delayed His coming.

Whereas the parable of the wedding banquet warned against rejecting the invitation and postponing preparation for the Messiah's coming, the parable of the ten virgins warns against being unprepared for the lengthy delay of the second coming of the Messiah. Since we do not know either the day or the hour of His second coming, how we live our lives every second, minute, hour, and day is important. We must be prepared at all times. Living for God isn't just a Sunday thing; it is an everyday thing. The King of kings is coming back. Will He find us ready and looking for His return?

Waiting for the return of Jesus Christ, our Messiah and Master, requires persistence, resistance to the influence of the world, determination, and constant vigilance of our spiritual condition. We must never tire of waiting for His return but be active in using our gifts and talents to extend God's kingdom to the ends of the earth.

The Parable of the Talents

After teaching His disciples about the unknown day of His second coming through the parable of the ten virgins, Jesus shared another parable with His disciples in Matthew 25:14–30:

> For it is just like a man going on a journey. He called his own slaves and turned over his possessions to them.

The Parables of the Kingdom

To one he gave five talents; to another, two; and to another, one—to each according to his own ability. Then he went on a journey. Immediately the man who had received five talents went, put them to work, and earned five more. In the same way the man with two earned two more. But the man who had received one talent went off, dug a hole in the ground, and hid his master's money.

After a long time the master of those slaves came and settled accounts with them. The man who had received five talents approached, presented five more talents, and said, 'Master, you gave me five talents. Look, I've earned five more talents.'

His master said to him, 'Well done, good and faithful slave! You were faithful over a few things; I will put you in charge of many things. Share your master's joy!'

"Then the man with two talents also approached. He said, 'Master, you gave me two talents. Look, I've earned two more talents.'

His master said to him, 'Well done, good and faithful slave! You were faithful over a few things; I will put you in charge of many things. Share your master's joy!'

Then the man who had received one talent also approached and said, 'Master, I know you. You're a difficult man, reaping where you haven't sown and gathering where you haven't scattered seed. So I was afraid and went off and hid your talent in the ground. Look, you have what is yours.'

But his master replied to him, 'You evil, lazy slave! If you knew that I reap where I haven't sown and gather where I haven't scattered, then you should have deposited my money with the bankers. And when I returned I would have received my money back with interest.

'So take the talent from him and give it to the one who has 10 talents. For to everyone who has, more will be given, and he will have more than enough. But from the one who does not have, even what he has will be taken away from him. And throw this good-for-nothing slave into the outer darkness. In that place there will be weeping and gnashing of teeth.'

With the parable of the talents, Jesus encouraged the disciples to use the gifts and resources God had entrusted to them to bring fruit into the kingdom of God as they waited for His return. A single talent was a very sizable sum of money.

In the parable, the man who went on the long journey symbolizes Jesus and the lengthy delay that will precede His glorious second coming. He gave His slaves talents according to their abilities. Both the one who received the five talents and the one who received two talents immediately invested their talents and made some gains, or profits, for their master, but the one who received one talent had some fear issues. Unwilling to invest the money, he dug a hole in the ground and hid his master's money.

After a long time, the master finally returned. The slaves

The Parables of the Kingdom

who had invested the talents reported their gains to their master, and to each one the master said, "Well done, good and faithful slave! You were faithful over a few things; I will put you in charge of many things. Share your master's joy!" (verse 23). However, to the fearful slave, the master said, "You evil, lazy slave! If you knew that I reap where I haven't sown and gather where I haven't scattered, then you should have deposited my money with the bankers. And when I returned I would have received my money back with interest" (verses 26–27). The master commanded that the talent be taken away from him and given to the one who had been given the five talents and had earned five more.

The point Jesus was driving home was that the disciples were to put their gifts and resources to use to bring fruit into the kingdom of God as they awaited His return. They were not to sit idly by or just go through the motions until He returned; they were to keep preaching the message their Master preached, and that message was about the goodness of the kingdom of God.

Jesus' return may seem to be delayed, but the truth is He is coming back. Use your time, talents, gifts, and money to win souls and bring fruit into the kingdom of God. Fear of man should never stop you from using your God-given gifts for the expansion of His kingdom. Remember, you personally will give an account of how you used the gifts and talents God gave you. Will God say to you, "Well done, good and faithful [servant]," or will He call you an "evil, lazy [servant]"?

Chapter 18

The Kingdom of God has come "Near You"

The parables of the kingdom illustrate how God's kingdom operates. Through the parables, we have seen God's kingdom revealed and demonstrated by Jesus in a very powerful and unique way. We are now going to take a closer look at what Jesus the Messiah meant when He said the kingdom of heaven has arrived, or has come near. We will also look at what the kingdom of God meant to ancient Israel at the time Jesus began to minister and proclaim the arrival of God's kingdom.

The Kingdom of Heaven Is Here Now!

Jesus not only preached the kingdom of God but also said something about its timing.

> "The time promised by God has come at last!" he announced. "The Kingdom of God is near! Repent of your sins and believe the Good News!" (Mark 1:15 NLT)

"When you enter any town, and they welcome you, eat

The Parables of the Kingdom

the things set before you. Heal the sick who are there, and tell them, 'The kingdom of God has come near you.'" (Luke 10:8-9)

What did Jesus mean when He said the kingdom "is near," or "has come near you"? In order to understand this expression, we need to go back to the Hebrew language of the Old Testament, with which Jesus, of course, was very familiar.

If we try to understand Luke 10:8-9 through a Greek mind-set or point of view, we will fail to understand the meaning of Jesus' words. In Hebrew, "to come near" (*karav*) really means "to be at." The Greek word equivalent of the Hebrew word *karav* is *engiken*. *Engiken*, however, does not mean quite the same thing as the Hebrew word *karav*. It simply means, "about to appear" or "almost here." The Greek *engiken*, like the English *near*, means "it is not yet here." The implication is that the kingdom of God is future—not yet here. However, the Hebrew *karav* means the exact opposite: "It is here! It has arrived."[13]

So, while Luke 10:9 uses *engiken* (i.e., "it is near"), which is the nearest Greek equivalent, the Hebrew concept of *karav* (i.e., "it is here") seems to convey the underlying meaning. The kingdom of heaven, or the kingdom of God, is always present tense—"right now." The kingdom of God is here now.[14]

One of the most powerful revelations in the teachings of Jesus is that the kingdom of heaven is here now, even though it is not yet here in its fullness (Matthew 4:17). The kingdom of heaven is not a political power, and it cannot and will not be established by human effort. It is not reserved only for the

---

13 David Bivin and Roy Blizzard Jr., *Understanding the Difficult Words of Jesus*, revised edition (Shippensburg, PA: Destiny Image, 1994), 62.
14 Ibid., 63.

distant future. It does not begin in the next millennium. For Jesus, the kingdom of heaven is here now.

The term *kingdom of heaven* or *kingdom of God* is used over one hundred times in the New Testament alone, yet most Christians today do not talk about it, and most preachers do not preach about it. In fact, they often dismiss it by saying that we are in the "church age" and must wait for Christ to return and set up His kingdom. Postponing the kingdom of heaven to a future age is simply postponing the power and dominion of the kingdom of heaven.

The kingdom of heaven is here now. It is here to influence, impact, and transform mankind's nature and character into the nature and character of God. In order to experience the influence and effect of the kingdom of heaven here on earth and in our lives, we must first welcome and receive it in our hearts.

Many people's idea of the kingdom of heaven is of some faraway "paradise" they will go to after death. Many people also believe the kingdom of heaven is not here yet because they cannot see it. Many have been taught to believe that the kingdom of heaven will come exploding down out of the clouds, with Jesus sitting upon an earthly throne. They are waiting for a rapture event to take them up into the heavens so they can finally be with Jesus and experience His kingdom.

The kingdom of God is not a place or a location; it is something spiritual, and it is within every believer in Christ (Luke 17:20–21). The kingdom of heaven is God's government ruling over people's hearts, minds, and spirits, influencing their actions, attitudes, and decisions. The kingdom of heaven is here now, even though we cannot physically touch it or see it. However, we definitely can see its influence and power over the lives of many believers in Christ and in all those who have been miraculously healed and delivered from sickness. We do not

The Parables of the Kingdom

have to wait for an event to take place so that we can experience God's kingdom. We can experience God's kingdom here and now.

Just as no one can see the wind when it is blowing yet we can feel its force and impact, the kingdom of heaven is unseen to the eye but we can certainly see its influence and impact upon the hearts of men and women around the world. As it blows the breath of life upon this earth, it changes stony hearts and causes people to return to their heavenly Father, just as the prodigal son in Jesus' parable returned to his father.

Yes, Jesus will return one day to reign over a perfect kingdom, where all evil and sin will be destroyed, but believers do not have to wait for a perfect world in order to begin living for God now. Many people are still looking for a physical kingdom to appear, without realizing the kingdom of heaven has already arrived and is here. It is operating right now, here on earth, through the power of the Holy Spirit, who is in the hearts of believers.

The kingdom of heaven began here on earth when God sent His Son to earth as a man in the person of Jesus. Today, Jesus Christ should be the reigning force in the hearts and minds of believers everywhere, because the kingdom of heaven is within us. Revelation 5:10 tells us that Jesus has made us a kingdom and priests to our God and that we will reign on the earth. We are called to reign here on earth and not to escape to some place because of evil on earth. Evil has no power over God's people. The apostle Paul writes in Colossians 1:13 that God has delivered us from the dominion of darkness and brought us into the kingdom of His beloved Son. The word *kingdom* in this verse does not refer to a territory but to the authority, rule, or sovereign power of a king. As a people who have been brought into the kingdom of God, we have the power to rule and reign with God here on earth.

How Do We Know the Kingdom of Heaven Is Here Now?

What is the evidence that the kingdom of heaven is here now?

- **We know that the kingdom of heaven is here now when sinners accept Jesus Christ and give their lives to him.**

No one here on earth is able to change his own sinful life and victoriously live for God in his own power. The hidden and yet visible influence of the kingdom of heaven here on earth gives God's people the power to break free from the bondage of sin to enter a life of freedom in Christ.

- **We know that the kingdom of heaven is here now when God's people freely forgive those who offend them** (like the prodigal son's father in Luke 15:11–32).

Forgiveness is not an easy thing. No one is able to genuinely forgive and forget the trespasses of another person by his own natural power. The power of God alone can and does empower people to forgive others and walk in love.

- **We know that the kingdom of heaven is here now when sick and demonically possessed people are delivered** (Matthew 14:34–36, 17:18).

There is no power or medication that can heal a demonically possessed person; only God's power can set people free from demonic oppression. Jesus' mighty miracles proved that

The Parables of the Kingdom

the kingdom of heaven had arrived. Healing is always evident wherever the kingdom of heaven is present.

- **We know that the kingdom of heaven is here now when God's people genuinely love others unconditionally** (Mark 12:31).

We know the kingdom of heaven is here when we see God's people loving others as Jesus did—unconditionally. Love for one another always demonstrates the presence of the kingdom of God in the hearts of believers.

The word *love* is very easy to say, but it is difficult to walk in love and live out love in our lives. Only the power of God can empower people to love others. Jesus demonstrated through the parables of the lost sheep (Matthew 18:10–14), the prodigal son (Luke 15:11–32), the friend in need (Luke 11:5–8), the good Samaritan (Luke 10:25–37), and the workers in the vineyard (Matthew 20:1–16) what true love is. Love for others, regardless of their background, is the evidence of the arrival and influence of the kingdom of heaven here on earth and in God's people.

True love is unconditional; it comes with no strings attached. When we see God's people choosing—contrary to human nature—to love others unconditionally, just as Jesus did, then we know the kingdom of heaven is here.

The Miracles of Healing

Healing is one of the most visible evidences of the presence of God's kingdom here on earth. Each time we hear of, or see, someone healed, we should remember that the kingdom of heaven is here now. Jesus preached the kingdom as

God's power on earth. The general theme of Jesus' parables was "the kingdom of heaven." His mighty miracles were intended to prove that the kingdom of God had arrived, not as people expected and not only in words, but with power. We know the kingdom of heaven is here now because people have experienced it. Their lives are not the same. They have been touched by the power of God's kingdom.

In Matthew 12:28, Jesus said, "If I drive out demons by the Spirit of God, then the kingdom of God has come to you." The kingdom of God was inaugurated, though not completely realized in its fullness, in the earthly ministry of Jesus Christ.

The kingdom principles from the life and teachings of Jesus demonstrate God's love, forgiveness, and acceptance. All people can experience God's rule when they obey God's absolutes. Healing, love, forgiveness, and acceptance are channels of God's power in a hurting world. God's saving activity establishes His kingdom now.

The power of the kingdom of heaven is here to influence every living being on earth, and it calls people to model love, forgiveness, mercy, and acceptance by following the example of Jesus. The parables, such as the parable of the prodigal son, teach God's people to walk in forgiveness and mercy. Christians should be a light to the lost and demonstrate the love of God to the nations.

The Light of the World

Let's change gears for a moment and take a look at Matthew 5:14–15: "You are the light of the world. A city situated on a hill cannot be hidden. No one lights a lamp and puts it under a basket, but rather on a lampstand, and it gives light for all who are in the house." The same thought is also presented in Mark 4:21–22, Luke 8:16, and Luke 11:33.

The typical lamp in a Jewish home was fairly small and was placed openly on a stand to give maximum illumination to the entire room. To the world, Christians are the light of the kingdom of heaven. They are called by God to display the light of His Spirit to those still living in darkness. Christians are the salt of the earth, bringing the flavor of the kingdom of heaven to the earth by healing the sick, setting the oppressed free, giving hope to the hopeless, and speaking life to the lifeless.

Christians are called by God to be ambassadors of His kingdom, representing His kingdom here on earth to every person, tribe, and nation. That means healing the sick, preaching the good news of the kingdom, loving others, and helping the needy. As God's ambassadors or representatives, what we do or say will bring either honor and glory to the kingdom of God or dishonor and shame. That is why it is important to keep our heart right and to guard against evil influence. We do not belong to ourselves anymore but to the creator of the heavens and the earth.

Facts about the Arrival of the Kingdom of Heaven

We can briefly summarize the biblical facts about the kingdom of heaven with the following list:
- The kingdom of heaven has arrived in an unexpected way.
- It has arrived in a mysterious manner.
- It began humbly through Jesus Christ.
- People can resist it.
- It is not a military kingdom, as many people expected.

- It is a spiritual kingdom.
- Its citizens must coexist with unbelievers for now, until Christ returns.
- It has arrived but not yet in the fullness of its glory and power.
- It dwells in the hearts of believers in Christ.
- It is a present spiritual reality, and it is not of the world.
- All men and women are invited to enter it.

Chapter 19

The Rule and Reign of God

Jesus' Primary Message

The dominant theme in the Gospels and the center of Jesus' proclamation was the reign or kingdom of God. This one phrase sums up his whole ministry and his whole life's work. Every thought and saying of Jesus was directed and subordinated to one single thing: the realization of the reign of God upon the earth.[15]

Before Jesus was crucified, He preached only the good news of the kingdom. After His resurrection, He continued to preach the message of the kingdom of God:

To them He showed Himself to be alive after His suffering through many convincing proofs, appearing to them for forty days and speaking about the kingdom of God. (Acts 1:3 Tree of Life Bible)

According to this Scripture, the only message Jesus preached

---

15 Kurt Struckmeyer, "The Reign of God" http://followingjesus.org/vision/reign_god.htm

after His resurrection concerned God's kingdom. His coming inaugurated the kingdom of God. When Jesus Christ returned to heaven, God's kingdom remained in the hearts of all believers through the presence of the Holy Spirit. However, as we have discussed already, the kingdom of God will not be fully realized until Jesus Christ returns. Until that time, we are to work to spread the good news of the kingdom to all the nations.

Jesus Preached the Kingdom-of-God Message

Here is a list of Scriptures that strongly show that Jesus preached only the kingdom of God: Matthew 4:17, 23; 5:3; 6:33; 13:11, 18–19, 24, 33, 44–45; 16:19, 27–28; 23:13; Luke 4:43; 9:11; 12:32; 16:16; John 18:36; Acts 1:3.

The term *kingdom*, as used by the Jews, often stressed the abstract idea of "reign" or "dominion," not some geographical area marked off by physical boundaries. The kingdom of heaven (or kingdom of God) is wherever the reign or dominion of God is manifested here on earth. In one sense, the kingdom of God has always existed, as we see in Psalm 47:2 and 103:19.

The kingdom, or reign, of God is not found in the form of a physical kingdom. In John 18:35–36, Jesus stood before Pilate.

> Pilate replied, "Your own nation and the chief priests handed You over to me. What have You done?"
>
> "My kingdom is not of this world," said Jesus. "If My kingdom were of this world, My servants would fight, so that I wouldn't be handed over to the Jews. As it is, My kingdom does not have its origin here."

The Parables of the Kingdom

This Scripture clearly points out that the kingdom of heaven is not a physical kingdom but a spiritual kingdom. Most Jews in Jesus' day could not understand this; they thought the Messiah was coming to establish a physical kingdom that would give them political freedom.

In John 6:14–15, when the people saw the signs and wonders Jesus had done, they wanted to come and take Him by force and make Him king, but He withdrew from that area and went to the mountain. Jesus did not come to establish a physical kingdom but to establish the rule and reign of the kingdom of heaven. The kingdom of heaven is far more powerful than a physical, human kingdom.

> What made Jesus so unique was his conviction that the reign of God had already started happening. The fundamental message of Jesus' proclamation was the day of God's reign had now dawned. The things that many prophets and righteous people had long desired to see and hear were now present before the eyes and ears of all. God's reign is here, Jesus announced. Or at least it is so near at hand that signs of its activity are clearly visible.[16]

The signs of God's rule were present in the words and deeds of Jesus Himself. Jesus' healing and even eating with sinners were signs that God's reign had arrived. "In general terms, Jesus proclaimed as 'good news' that God was setting about the task of putting straight the evil plight into which the world had fallen, and that God was beginning to bring to fulfillment His original intention in the creation."[17]

---
16 Struckmeyer, "The Reign of God.".
17 Ibid.

It is amazing to see that many sick people recognized the arrival of the kingdom of heaven on earth in the ministry of Jesus. They recognized the kingship and power of Jesus over every infirmity and even His power to forgive sins. Some cried out to Him to have mercy on them (Luke 18:38), while others touched the hem of His garment (Mark 5:21–34), and the list goes on and on. The point is that we need to recognize God's kingship through His Son Jesus Christ.

God's kingdom begins to operate in people's lives when they realize His influence in their hearts and recognize that the kingdom of heaven is in their midst.

God's Kingship Is Recognized

The recitation of the Shema in rabbinic teaching was connected directly to the kingdom of heaven. When the Jewish people recite the Shema—"Listen, Israel: The Lord our God, the Lord is one" (Deuteronomy 6:4)—the Lord is declared king. The kingdom of heaven is realized, and one cannot simply go through the motions of saying the words. Each person must concentrate and direct his or her heart toward God.

To recognize that the kingdom of heaven is here is to recognize God's kingship and authority over our lives and to reject all idolatry. The parables of Jesus provide us with illustrations of the influence and power of the kingdom of heaven (reign and dominion) here on earth. The parables also help us to understand how the kingdom of heaven operates on earth.

The kingdom of God is revealed to the world through the influence and power it has in the Christian's lifestyle. A believer's actions, attitudes, and character prove to the world that God's kingdom is here now.

The good news of the kingdom is very important to the

body of Christ. The church has nothing to preach apart from the message of the kingdom. That message has the power to set captives free, heal the brokenhearted, and proclaim the year of the Lord's favor (Isaiah 61:1–2; Luke 4:18–19).

The good news of the kingdom is what can and will give Christians the power to live for God here on earth. The apostle Paul wrote in 1 Corinthians 4:20, "The Kingdom of God is not just a lot of talk; it is living by God's power" (NLT). God's people cannot walk in God's power without first accepting the influence of the kingdom of heaven in their hearts.

The Ever-Increasing Kingdom

Matthew 11:12 says, "From the days of John the Baptist until now, the kingdom of heaven has been suffering violence, and the violent have been seizing it by force."

Many Bible scholars consider Matthew 11:12 one of the most difficult and most misunderstood verses in the Bible. Does it suggest that the kingdom of God is under attack or has been under attack? What does "suffering violence" really mean, and how is it related to the kingdom of heaven and to the mission of Jesus? Certainly, the kingdom of heaven's "suffering violence" does not mean God's kingdom is under attack by violent or powerful people and that Christians must defend it by force or the use of violence.

There are several different views concerning the interpretation of Matthew 11:12:

- Jesus may have been referring to a vast movement toward God, the momentum of which began with John's preaching.
- Jesus may have been reflecting the Jewish activists'

expectation that God's kingdom would come through a violent overthrow of Rome.

- Jesus may have meant that entering God's kingdom takes courage, unwavering faith, determination, and endurance because of the growing opposition leveled at Jesus' followers.
- "Suffering violence" may indicate opposition from the religious establishment, with the violent attacking probably referring to the actions of specific evil people such as Herod Antipas, who had arrested John.

All these suggestions sound reasonable, but Brad H. Young's suggestion about Matthew 11:12 makes a lot of sense. He suggests that rather than "suffering violence," the phrase should be translated "forcefully advancing" (NLT) or, even better, "breaking forth." Thus, the expression does not mean violent men are attacking the kingdom of heaven but that the kingdom is forcefully advancing or powerfully breaking forth.[18]

The *NIV Study Bible* notes that the verb can be taken in either an active or a passive sense. If taken passively, it means the kingdom is under attack, and it would emphasize the "ongoing persecution of the people of the kingdom."[19] If taken in the active sense, it means the opposite: that the kingdom of God is forcefully advancing.

Yes, Christians around the world suffer persecution, but that does not mean the kingdom of God is under attack. The kingdom of God, in fact, would presumably be too powerful to be under attack. Therefore, it would seem best to follow Young

---

18 Young, *Jesus the Jewish Theologian*, 50–52.
19 Kenneth L. Barker, gen. ed., *The NIV Study Bible*, 2011 edition (Grand Rapids: Zondervan, 2011), 1611. See also, John Engler, "The Forceful Men in Matthew 11:12," http://www.barnabasministry.com/seminary-passages-matthew1112.pdf.

here and take this to mean that the kingdom of God is forcefully advancing.

Messianic Expectations in the First Century

Recent research by Jewish-roots-focused Bible scholars shows that to understand the context and meaning of Matthew 11:12, one must first study all the verses of Matthew 11 and have some knowledge about the first-century messianic expectation. In Matthew 11, we see that from prison John the Baptist sent a message by his disciples to Jesus, asking, "Are you the Messiah we've been expecting, or should we keep looking for someone else?" (Matthew 11:3 NLT). The question reflects the messianic expectation of the Jewish people of Jesus' day.

The messianic expectations are critical to the popular and official evaluation of the kingdom message Jesus preached. Various messianic expectations abounded in the first century. Several different themes came together from various prophecies. The first of these was the idea of a Davidic ruler who would usher in the day of the Lord (Isaiah 9:6; 11:1).

Another expression of this hope was the Servant of the Lord (Isaiah 49:3–6). The promises of a Prince from the house of David who would break the oppressor's yoke from His people's neck seemed to many to be designed for a time such as John the Baptist's, whether the yoke was imposed by a Herodian ruler or by a Roman governor. In Matthew 11, we see that Herod had imprisoned John, and John needed some answers from Yeshua. He sent his questions to Jesus through his disciples.

John the Baptist's own expectations of the work of the Messiah are very important in this passage. His question "Are you the Messiah?" arises from John's "Jewish" expectation of a military Messiah. The hope of a "military Messiah" dominated the Jewish community of Jesus' day, and John's thinking as well, as we can tell by his question to Jesus.

Many Jewish people expected the Messiah to expel the Romans and supersede the existing religious authorities in Israel. However, Jesus focused His attention on needy and receptive hearts, rather than on confronting or overthrowing unreceptive authorities.

While John himself suffered imprisonment, it doesn't appear the *kingdom* itself had really suffered from violence. The whole point of Jesus' remarks in Matthew 11:4–6 is that the kingdom had been advancing just fine even though John was in prison; it had not been thwarted. In fact, in Matthew 11:5, Jesus gave John's disciples proof of how God's kingdom was forcefully advancing:

- The blind see
- The lame walk
- Those with skin diseases are healed
- The deaf hear
- The dead are raised
- The poor are told the good news

After John the Baptist had made the way for Him, Jesus' ministry dynamically advanced as a force for healing and wholeness in a suffering world. The kingdom of heaven cannot suffer violence; rather, it is breaking forth (Micah 2:13).

It is important to understand, however, that in Matthew 11:12 Jesus was not teaching force as an acceptable method of operation in God's kingdom. He was not encouraging Christians to be aggressive toward anyone who rejects the kingdom of heaven. The kingdom cannot be imposed upon others through violence. The kingdom of God is the power

The Parables of the Kingdom

of God at work to help people, not destroy them. Jesus and John both advanced the kingdom, yet they were subject to criticism arising from superficial public expectations and perceptions of the kingdom. Through it all, they did not turn to violence as a way of advancing God's kingdom, and neither did they advocate it.

The progress of the kingdom of heaven here on earth is not about physical or "forceful" proclamations, overthrowing sinful religious or civic leaders, or taking over the world militarily. The breaking forth of the kingdom of heaven is spiritual, not physical. Believers in Christ should never use Matthew 11:12 to justify violence toward unbelievers.

The kingdom of heaven expands and advances by the power of the Holy Spirit; it does not expand or advance by way of physical force or power or the will of man. Despite all the failures by men and women of God around the world, the kingdom of heaven is still breaking forth, and no one can stop it.

In the parables of the mustard seed and the leaven, Jesus described the reign of God as a force in the present world that progressively grows. He commanded His disciples to go into all the world and preach the good news of the kingdom (Mark 16:15). He also commissioned them to go and make disciples of all nations, baptizing them in the name of the Father, the Son, and the Holy Spirit (Matthew 28:19).

Jesus' disciples were to baptize people because baptism symbolically unites believers with the kingdom of heaven and with Jesus Christ. Baptism symbolizes submission to the King, Jesus Christ, and to God's kingdom. It also shows a person's willingness to be influenced by the kingdom of heaven.

Dr. Kazumba Charles

The Kingdom of God in Its Fullness

The kingdom of heaven has a future element as well. The fullness of the kingdom will be unveiled at the second coming of Jesus. In Matthew 25:34, Jesus spoke of this future aspect, when God's people will finally inherit the fullness of the kingdom of heaven. The future coming of the kingdom of heaven is also spoken of in 1 Corinthians 15:50–57, 2 Timothy 4:18, and 2 Peter 1:10–11.

Peter described the coming of the kingdom of God in its fullness in 2 Peter 3:10–13. The fullness of the kingdom of heaven will embrace the new heavens and new earth. The good news, however, is that we do not have to wait to experience the kingdom of heaven; the kingdom of heaven is here now; so we can experience it right now, not just in the future.

The church should never postpone God's kingdom to a future date. The kingdom of heaven is here now, even though it is not yet experienced in its fullness. Wherever the sovereignty of God is accepted in the hearts of men and women, there the kingdom of heaven is. In the future, the fullness of the kingdom of heaven will be "culminated" with the second coming of the Messiah, Yeshua.

In 1 Corinthians 15:20–24 Paul writes,

> But now Christ has been raised from the dead, the firstfruits of those who have fallen asleep. For since death came through a man, the resurrection of the dead also comes through a man. For as in Adam all die, so also in Christ all will be made alive. But each in his own order: Christ, the firstfruits; afterward, at His coming, those who belong to Christ. Then comes the end, when He hands over the kingdom to God the

Father, when He abolishes all rule and all authority and power.

The Bible does not give us the specific day, time, month, and year when Yeshua will hand over the kingdom of heaven to God the Father. No one knows when the kingdom of heaven will come in fullness. Paul points out in 1 Corinthians 15:24 that the resurrected Christ will conquer all evil, including death. When the fullness of God's kingdom is revealed, there will be no more death, and the righteous will shine forth as the sun in the kingdom of their Father (Matthew 13:43).

Still, to focus solely on the end-time events is to deny the power of God's kingdom that Jesus revealed to the world.

The Kingdom of God Is Within Us

Luke 17:20–21 records Jesus' reply to a question of the Pharisees about when the kingdom of God will come. Jesus answered, "The kingdom of God is not coming with something observable; no one will say, 'Look here!' or 'There!' For you see, the kingdom of God is among you."

The Jewish people of Jesus' day were looking for the kingdom of God to come with signs in the sky and miracles. In this passage, Jesus made it very clear that the kingdom of God is in the hearts of people. In Luke 17:20–21, Jesus described the kingdom's coming as being unobservable. In fact, Scripture tells us that the kingdom of heaven was present in spiritual form on earth, as demonstrated by Christ's ability to cast out demons, heal, and save (Matthew 4:23; 12:28).

The Gospels focus on the present aspect of the kingdom of God with Jesus on earth. But it is also clear that they speak of the kingdom that will be realized in the future at the second coming of Jesus Christ to earth. Christ will return to establish His kingdom in its fully realized form, and the righteous will shine like the sun, thus reflecting the glory of God. However, we do not have to wait for the arrival of the fullness of the kingdom here on earth in order to shine like the sun and reflect the glory of God. The kingdom of heaven is here. It has come early for us, and we can reflect the glory of God and shine like the sun *now*, by accepting the rule and reign of God in our hearts.

Entering the Kingdom of Heaven

How can a person enter the kingdom of heaven? Is entrance to the kingdom of heaven limited only to one religious group or to a certain denomination? To help us find the answers to these questions, let's turn to John 3. Here we see a Jewish ruler by the name of Nicodemus, who came to Jesus at night.

> This man . . . said, "Rabbi, we know that You have come from God as a teacher, for no one could perform these signs You do unless God were with him."
>
> Jesus replied, "I assure you: Unless someone is born again, he cannot see the kingdom of God."
>
> "But how can anyone be born when he is old?"
>
> Nicodemus asked Him. "Can he enter his mother's womb a second time and be born?"
>
> Jesus answered, "I assure you: Unless someone is born of water and the Spirit, he cannot enter the kingdom of

The Parables of the Kingdom

God. Whatever is born of the flesh is flesh, and whatever is born of the Spirit is spirit." (John 3:2–6)

According to Jesus, in order for a person to enter, or inherit, the kingdom of heaven, he or she must be born again. Jesus explained to Nicodemus that his physical birth ("of the flesh") was one thing and the spiritual birth ("of the Spirit") was an entirely different thing. To enter the kingdom of heaven, one must be born of the Spirit through faith in Jesus. Jesus is the only way to the Father; no one can enter the kingdom of heaven by any means other than faith in Jesus Christ (see John 14:6).

In John 3:3, Jesus taught that to enter the kingdom of God one must be "born again," or born of God. Being born into this world is our first birth, and no one is given any choice in that matter. However, God gives us the choice of having a second birth, which allows us to start a new life in Him.

What Does Being "Born Again" Mean?

The Bible does not give us a succinct definition of being born again. Many Bible scholars translate the phrase "born again" as "born from above." This translation, which is certainly possible, emphasizes that this birth comes only from the Spirit and power of God. Being born again is an act of God whereby eternal life is imparted to the person who believes in Jesus Christ (2 Corinthians 5:17; Titus 3:5; 1 Peter 1:3; 1 John 2:29; 5:1–4).[20] To be born again is simply to have a new birth in Christ and to allow the kingdom of heaven to influence our life.

---

20   Got Questions Ministries, "What does it mean to be a born again Christian?" http://www.gotquestions.com/born-again.html

Enter by the Narrow Gate

In Matthew 7:13, Jesus said that in order for a person to enter the kingdom of heaven, he or she must enter through the narrow gate. The wide gate and broad road lead to destruction. Jesus was not suggesting that it is extremely difficult to inherit, or enter, the kingdom of heaven; rather, He was emphasizing that there is only one way that leads to the kingdom of heaven and that only a few decide to take that narrow path. The way that leads to the kingdom of heaven requires a single focus, a single desire, and a single mind-set.

The "narrow gate" symbolizes the exclusive nature of the kingdom of heaven. Entrance into the kingdom of heaven requires the disciple of Jesus to do the will of the Father in heaven. Jesus said, "Not everyone who says to Me, 'Lord, Lord!' will enter the kingdom of heaven, but only the one who does the will of My Father in heaven" (Matthew 7:21).

To enter the kingdom of heaven, one must have childlike humility.

> At that time the disciples came to Jesus and said, "Who is greatest in the kingdom of heaven?"
>
> Then He called a child to Him and had him stand among them. "I assure you," He said, "unless you are converted and become like children, you will never enter the kingdom of heaven. Therefore, whoever humbles himself like this child—this one is the greatest in the kingdom of heaven. And whoever welcomes one child like this in My name welcomes Me." (Matthew 18:1–5)

The Parables of the Kingdom

These verses are commonly used to promote childlike innocence or naivety. However, a careful study shows that Jesus' statement, "unless you are converted and become like children," was actually urging His disciples to adopt childlike humility. Humility is the path to true greatness in the kingdom of heaven, and God loves the humble. Proverbs 3:34 says, "He mocks those who mock, but gives grace to the humble."

People of humility will inherit the kingdom of heaven because they are quick to humble themselves before God and before others when they have missed the mark. Humble people repent quickly and seek to maintain their relationship with God and others.

A proud person never accepts that he is wrong; he cannot admit he is a sinner who needs repentance. The humble in heart know the importance of repentance, while the proud in heart do not.

For God to reign powerfully in the heart of a person, a change must take place in that person's heart. Change takes place when a person hears the good news of the kingdom, repents of his sins, and accepts Jesus Christ as his Lord and Savior. Repentance is simply changing the direction our life is going and doing the will of God. Man is lost in sin; his heart is corrupt in nature, and therefore he cannot save himself by his own efforts. His heart must be changed by God.

To enter the kingdom of heaven, a person must have a new heart and a new spirit in him.

> I will give you a new heart and put a new spirit within you; I will remove your heart of stone and give you a heart of flesh. (Ezekiel 36:26)

Who Is Greatest in the Kingdom of Heaven?

Let us look again at the first few verses in Matthew 18:

At that time the disciples came to Jesus and said, "Who is greatest in the kingdom of heaven?"

Then He called a child to Him and had him stand among them. "I assure you," He said, "unless you are converted and become like children, you will never enter the kingdom of heaven. Therefore, whoever humbles himself like this child—this one is the greatest in the kingdom of heaven."

Note the question that elicited Jesus' comments about childlike humility. The disciples of Jesus asked Him who would be the greatest in the kingdom of heaven. It is clear from their question that the disciples misunderstood greatness in terms of human endeavor, accomplishment, and status. The kingdom of heaven is not about these things, however. Jesus used a child to make His point to the self-centered disciples.

Jesus explained that whoever humbles himself like a child is the greatest in the kingdom of heaven. Humility is the way to true greatness and key to entering the kingdom of heaven. Human achievement or status does not count with Jesus; humility is what moves the heart of God. People become great in God's sight as they sincerely and humbly look away from serving self to serving God and His created people (Mark 10:43). The life of discipleship is characterized by humble and loving service.

The greatest in the kingdom of heaven are those who are

The Parables of the Kingdom

humble like children. The humility of a child consists of trust, vulnerability, and recognition that one is unable to advance his or her own cause apart from the help, direction, and resources of a parent. When we are humble before God, trusting in His ability and power, God will empower us to do greater things for Him. The greatest is the one who serves others and is willing to suffer on their behalf. Being humble does not mean walking the street with our head down. Being humble is simply being able to recognize our own shortcomings rather than hiding them and being able to repent before God.

To enter the kingdom of heaven, now and in the future, a person

- Must be born again (John 3:3)
- Must be born of the Spirit (John 3:5)
- Must be born of water (John 3:5)
- Must have childlike humility (Matthew 18:3)
- Must enter through the narrow gate (Matthew 7:13)
- Must believe in Jesus (John 14:6)
- Must enter by God's grace alone (Eph. 2:8–9)

Chapter 20

A Brief Summary

What Is the Kingdom of Heaven Like?

In the Gospels, Jesus does not give us a specific, dictionary definition of the kingdom of heaven, but He does describe what the kingdom of heaven is like by using simple, yet powerful, illustrations known as parables.

In summary, those parables teach that the kingdom of heaven is like the following:

- A man who sowed good seed in his field, but while his men were sleeping, his enemy came and sowed weeds among the wheat. When the plants came up and bore grain, then the weeds appeared also (Matthew 13:24–26).
- A mustard seed that a man took and planted in his field. Though it is the smallest of all seeds, when it grows up, it is the largest of the garden plants and becomes a tree (Matthew 13:31–32).
- Yeast that a woman took and mixed into a large amount of flour until it worked all through the dough (Matthew 13:33).

The Parables of the Kingdom

- Treasure hidden in a field (Matthew 13:44).
- A merchant looking for fine pearls (Matthew 13:45).
- A net that was let down into the lake and caught all kinds of fish (Matthew 13:47).
- A king who wanted to settle accounts with his servants (Matthew 18:23).
- A landowner who went out early in the morning to hire men to work in his vineyard (Matthew 20:1).
- A king who prepared a wedding banquet for his son (Matthew 22:2).

A third of the recorded teachings of Jesus in the Synoptic Gospels are in the form of parables. In fact, according to Mark 4:34, Jesus did not teach the masses without using parables. In order to understand Jesus' teaching about the kingdom of heaven, one must carefully study the parables and understand their messages. Parables illustrate the activities of the kingdom of heaven here on earth.

From this study, it is clear that the focus of Jesus' preaching and teaching was on the kingdom of God. It is important to understand that Jesus did not preach any message other than the kingdom-of-heaven message. Through His parables, He revealed the nature and character of God and His kingdom. He also demonstrated what the kingdom of heaven is like and how it operates, in contrast to the expectations of the people of His day.

The kingdom of heaven is not a geographic location but a spiritual kingdom where God rules and where we share in His kingdom, both now and in the future. God's kingdom is here now, even though it is not yet here in its fullness. The miraculous healings of Yeshua in the Gospels announced the arrival of the kingdom of heaven here on earth.

Again, if we desire to know more about the nature and character of God and His kingdom, we must study the parables of the kingdom. Not only do the parables teach us about God's nature and character, but they also inspire us to change the way we view God and His created people. The kingdom principles from the life and teachings of Jesus demonstrate God's love, forgiveness, and acceptance. Through the parables of the kingdom, we see the grace, mercy, love, forgiveness, and compassion of God. Those who share in His kingdom must demonstrate and exercise His character in their lives.

The parables make it very clear that the kingdom is present and at work in the world. God's kingdom is here, actively working among men and women and powerfully destroying the works of Satan; but in the present time, God will not force or compel people to bow before His kingdom. People must willingly receive it, and the response must come from a willing heart and submissive will.

The kingdom of God is a present reality (Matthew 12:28), and yet it is a future blessing (1 Corinthians 15:50). We enter the kingdom now through faith in Christ (Matthew 21:31), and yet we will enter it in its fullness in the future (Matthew 8:11).

Spiritual Applications of Jesus' Parables

There are many life-changing spiritual truths and applications we can gain from the parables of Jesus. Through the kingdom parables, Jesus taught important principles we need to know and understand about the nature, power, influence, and character of God's kingdom. If put into practice in our everyday lives, the principles Jesus taught in the parables can transform our lives and the lives of those around us. Let us now look at those spiritual applications of the good news of the kingdom that we find in the parables Jesus taught.

The Parable of the Sower

The Word of God begins to grow in the hearts of people only if their hearts are responsive to it. A person cannot grow spiritually if he or she does not respond wholeheartedly to the Word of God. It is the responsibility of every Christian to guard his or her heart from things that cause it to become stony and unresponsive ground. A person who receives the Word with a good heart and puts it into practice will bear much fruit in the kingdom. The one who does not receive the Word with a good heart will never bear much fruit. Salvation is more than a superficial experience. The seed of salvation that has been planted in the heart of every believer in Christ must be allowed to produce good fruit.

One thing that hinders many of us Christians from walking in the power and influence of the kingdom of God—that is, being "good soil"—is the cares of this world. The pursuit of riches and a strong desire for pleasure weaken our spiritual lives and destroy our focus on God. No one can serve two masters at the same time. Jesus said, "No one can be a slave of two masters, since either he will hate one and love the other, or be devoted to one and despise the other. You cannot be slaves of God and of money" (Matthew 6:24).

It is not wrong to have riches or to have some pleasure and enjoy life. In fact, the Bible encourages us to enjoy life and the fruits of our labor (Psalm 128:2; Isaiah 62:9; Ecclesiastes 3:9–13). What is not pleasing to God is allowing riches and pleasure to take the center stage in our lives. God must always be number one in our lives, and we must pursue Him with everything within us.

A disciple's loyalties cannot be divided; he is a slave either to God or to the things of this world. Our loyalty should be to our King and Master, Jesus Christ, and to God's kingdom. As we value the rule and reign of God over our lives and diligently pursue righteous living, we can trust God to satisfy and meet our needs. In Matthew 6:33 Jesus said, "Seek first the kingdom of God and His righteousness, and all these things will be provided for you."

Seeking the kingdom of God above all else means putting God first and allowing Him to fill our thoughts with His desires and His kingdom principles. God's kingdom and nothing else must be our priority, and the cares of this world should never be allowed to compete with that priority.

Materialism and humanism also hinder our spiritual progress. These secular lifestyles choke the spiritual life out of us. This kind of spiritual death does not rush upon a person suddenly but occurs gradually. Spiritual weeds grow slowly, but in time they strangle the budding spiritual life that is there. According to the world's philosophy, "The person with the most toys wins." Sadly, however, the person who pursues "toys" dies spiritually. Jesus said, "What will it benefit a man if he gains the whole world yet loses His life?" (Matthew 16:26).

The parable of the sower should encourage all spiritual "farmers"—those who teach, preach, and seek to lead others to the Lord. The farmer sowed good seed, but not all the seed sprouted, and even the plants that grew had varying yields. Ministers of the good news of the kingdom should not be discouraged if they do not always see spiritual change in people. However, they must faithfully teach and minister the Word of

God, continuing to scatter the seed of the Word of God in the hearts of people. The Holy Spirit will do the rest.

No one has the power to spiritually change another person. Only the Spirit of God has that power. Yes, through the power of God, people can inspire others to live for God, but they can do only so much. The job of pastors and evangelists is to deliver the word of God into the hearts of people around the world and leave it up to the Holy Spirit to do the rest.

The Parable of the Wheat and the Weeds

According to Jesus' explanation of the parable of the wheat and the weeds, the "weeds" are the children of the Devil. The Devil sows them in the same field in which God sows His children ("good seed"). Any attempt to gather or uproot the weeds would only endanger the good wheat because the roots of the weeds become intertwined with those of the wheat. However, when harvesttime comes, the angels of the Lord will uproot them all and separate the wheat from the weeds.

This shows us that the children of God must live side by side with unbelievers in this life, until the fullness of the kingdom of God is revealed at the second coming of Jesus Christ. God allows both believers and unbelievers to live in the same world until the day of judgment. The Christian's job is to help unbelievers come to the Lord, not to condemn or judge them (Matthew 7:1–5).

Just as it is not easy to distinguish between wheat and weeds because they both look alike in the early stages of growth, it is not always easy in our world to distinguish between those who are truly children of God and those who merely *pretend* to belong to Him. Many, many people around the world claim to be children of God and claim to do things in His name or on His behalf, but God knows His own. He knows those who are His and those who are not.

Galatians 5:22–23 can help us test ourselves to see whether it is the "seed of the kingdom of God" that is operating in our lives rather than the seed of the Devil. God's seed produces love, joy, peace, patience, kindness, goodness, faithfulness, gentleness, self-control, and forgiveness, while the Devil's seed produces the very opposite of all these.

In Matthew 7:15–18 Jesus tells us,

> Beware of false prophets who come to you in sheep's clothing but inwardly are ravaging wolves. You'll recognize them by their fruit. Are grapes gathered from thornbushes or figs from thistles? In the same way, every good tree produces good fruit, but a bad tree produces bad fruit. A good tree can't produce bad fruit; neither can a bad tree produce good fruit.

God's people are recognized by their fruits and not by their religious acts. The influence and effect of the kingdom of heaven upon our lives should differentiate us from non-Christians and cause us to produce good fruit in all seasons. The reign and influence of God in our lives is seen visibly by others through the fruit of the Spirit operating in us, not by our Christian sweet talk or superspiritual attitudes and actions.

The Parables of the Mustard Seed and the Yeast

What can mustard seeds teach us about the kingdom of God? The tiny mustard seed literally grows to be a tree that attracts numerous birds to its branches. God's kingdom works in a similar fashion. It starts from the smallest beginnings in the hearts of men and women who are receptive to God's Word. It then works unseen, causing a transformation from within.

Just as a seed has no power to change itself into a plant or tree until it is planted in the ground (John 12:24), we too cannot change our lives to be like Jesus until we die to our old self and yield to Christ. Then God empowers us with the Holy Spirit who dwells in us. The kingdom of God transforms those who receive the new life Jesus Christ offers.

The slow beginning of the transformation in our lives should not discourage us. Just as a small mustard seed later grows into a tree, we too start our spiritual lives very slowly as we deal with past issues, but later we grow spiritually into mighty men and women of God. Every living thing here on earth grows in stages called "life cycles." Life has a course with a beginning, middle, and end. The same is true of our spiritual lives; we must allow the Holy Spirit to work in us in stages, realizing, of course, that our spiritual life has no end; indeed, not even death can end it.

The Power of Yeast

Just as yeast influences the whole batch of dough into which it is placed, the kingdom of heaven influences the entire life of any person who accepts it into his or her life. Likewise, when we accept the influence of the kingdom of heaven in our lives, we become like yeast to our friends and families, influencing them with the life of the kingdom. Jesus calls us to be like yeast in a positive way, influencing people with the good news of the kingdom. To influence people for God, we need only to have faith as tiny as a mustard seed. Faith in Jesus will allow us to be confident in sharing the Word of God with other people without fear.

Faith Like a Mustard Seed

Jesus told His disciples in Matthew 17:20, "If you have faith the size of a mustard seed, you will tell this mountain, 'Move from here to there,' and it will move. Nothing will be impossible for you."

The disciples of Jesus had failed to heal a demon-possessed boy who had seizures and suffered severely. In other words, they had failed to overcome the demonic power that was in that boy. When they asked Jesus why, He said it was because of their little faith. To be influential in the kingdom of heaven here on earth, we need to have faith, even if it is as tiny as a mustard seed. We cannot sow the seed (the Word of God) in the hearts of people without first having faith in the seed itself. Furthermore, we cannot bring people into the kingdom of God or heal and deliver them without faith in the Word of God.

Nothing Christ authorizes His followers to do is impossible with faith. If we have faith in Him, we can accomplish great things for the kingdom of God. The Word we preach and share with our friends and families has the power to turn their hearts and lives to God.

The Parable of the Growing Seed

The parable of the growing seed gives us a picture of how the kingdom of God grows. The seed is the Word of God. When the seed is sown in a person's heart, it grows into convictions that bring about change. This growing process, however, is not accomplished by the person but by God. God works

The Parables of the Kingdom

behind the scenes to develop and grow the seed. The apostle Paul was a sower. He wrote in 1 Corinthians 3:6–7, "I planted, Apollos watered, but God gave the growth. So then neither the one who plants nor the one who waters is anything, but only God who gives the growth."

This parable is not teaching that God saves people even if we do not share His Word with them or pray for them. It is teaching that as mere human beings we are sowers and waterers of the seed and tenders of the soil; we cannot create the phenomenon of growth because we do not have the power to cause the seed to bring forth the fruits of life. Only the creator of all things can give life; only He has the power over the seed. The job of a sower is to sow the seed in the ground and water it; it is Yahweh who gives life to that seed.

As laborers in the kingdom of God, our job is to plant the seed—the Word of God—in the hearts of people. It is God's job to change people's hearts of stone and draw them to Himself (John 12:32). Our witness to people with the message of the kingdom may not bring fast and quick results, but our efforts in sharing that powerful message definitely will influence people for God.

The parable of the growing seed teaches us about the unique power of the Word of God. Just as the natural seed has life in itself, so the Word of God is infused with life and power. The Word of God is a powerful growth agent that expands and grows the kingdom of heaven here on earth.

Jesus Christ gave life with just a word. Lazarus's body had been in the grave until it stank, but when Jesus said, "Lazarus, come out!" (John 11:43), Lazarus came forth! With just a word, Christ could curse the fig tree and take life from it. With a word He cast out demons, healed diseases, gave sight to the blind, and calmed the storm.

There is a unique power in the Word of God. We are saved—born again, born of the Spirit—because the Word of God was spoken and planted in our hearts by men and women of God. The apostle Peter writes in 1 Peter 1:23–25,

> You have been born again—not of perishable seed but of imperishable—through the living and enduring word of God. For all flesh is like grass, and all its glory like a flower of the grass. The grass withers, and the flower falls, but the word of the Lord endures forever.

We are born again, not of perishable seed (word), but of imperishable seed. The Word of God is imperishable. Once it is planted in a person's heart, it will gradually grow. It may not seem to grow right away, but it will grow and bring forth fruit. When a farmer sows his seed, he does so with the intention of reaping a harvest. The same is true of God. Jesus began to sow the seed of the Word of God (the good news of the kingdom) into the hearts of men and women two thousand years ago, and His church has continued to sow that seed ever since. The Bible says that one day, at God's appointed time, the earth will be harvested.

> Then I looked, and there was a white cloud, and One like the Son of Man was seated on the cloud, with a gold crown on His head and a sharp sickle in His hand. Another angel came out of the sanctuary, crying out in a loud voice to the One who was seated on the cloud, "Use your sickle and reap, for the time to reap has come, since the harvest of the earth is ripe." So the One seated on the cloud swung His sickle over the earth, and the earth was harvested. (Revelation 14:14–16)

The Parables of the Kingdom

This passage in Revelation tells us that on that day, the One who will do the harvesting is the Son of God, Jesus Christ. The crown of gold on His head indicates that He is King of kings and Lord of lords. Jesus, who was the first to sow the seeds of the kingdom of God on earth, will one day return to harvest His crop.

In the parable of the growing seed, *we* are the people planting the seed. Once we have planted the seed, we have no control over it. God is responsible for the seed's growth. This part of the parable is a good representation of our relationship with God. God does all the hard work. He is the One who makes the seed grow, but He still uses us to plant the seed.

It is also important to know that seeds grow slowly. When we spread the Word of God, we are probably not going to see results right away. Sometimes it will take a long time before the seed produces fruit. We might not even get to *see* the seed grow. But eventually the seed will grow, and the Word of God will spread.

The Parables of the Prodigal Son, the Lost Sheep, and the Lost Coin

Just as the older brother of the prodigal son did not like his father openly displaying his compassion and welcoming home his lost son, many self-centered Christians find it difficult to genuinely forgive and welcome their backslidden brothers or sisters into the church—even when they repent. Jonah displayed a similar attitude.

The Lord called Jonah to warn the Assyrians that they would suffer God's judgment if they did not repent. However, Jonah hated the powerful and wicked Assyrians and he knew deep down in his heart that, if he went to Nineveh and warned the Assyrians of the coming judgment of God upon them, they would respond to the message and repent. God would then forgive them and not punish them. So Jonah decided not to go to Nineveh. God, however, worked in a marvelous and supernatural way to get Jonah to Nineveh.

When Jonah preached the message to the people of Nineveh, they responded to the message (Jonah 3:5–9). When God saw that they repented and stopped their evil ways, He showed compassion to them and did not carry out the destruction He had threatened (verse 10).

When he saw God's mercy and compassion toward the wicked Assyrians, Jonah was very upset, just as the prodigal son's brother was upset when his father showed compassion to his runaway younger brother. Jonah complained to God and said:

> "Isn't this what I said while I was still in my own country? That's why I fled toward Tarshish in the first place. I knew that You are a merciful and compassionate God, slow to become angry, rich in faithful love, and One who relents from sending disaster" (Jonah 4:2).

Jonah was reluctant to go to Nineveh because he did not want the Ninevites forgiven; he wanted them destroyed. He forgot that the God of Israel was also the God who created the Assyrians. The older brother of the prodigal son also forgot that his father was still a father to his younger brother, even though the younger son had sinned against his father. He was upset because his father demonstrated unbelievable compassion to his younger brother.

As God's children, we need to remember always that our heavenly Father also has the love of a father for those who are

The Parables of the Kingdom

lost. He loves them just as He loves us, and He is waiting to welcome them into His kingdom. Our job and mandate is to inspire others to turn to God the Father, not condemn them to death. We are to go into all the nations and proclaim the compassion, mercy, and love of God.

When we see people who have abandoned God repent and return to Him, we should not get upset but rejoice with God and with all His angels. We should not act like the prodigal son's older brother or like Jonah. Rather, we should respond like the prodigal son's father, with a heart full of compassion, forgiveness, love, and mercy.

The kingdom of God is filled with love, forgiveness, mercy, and restoration for all sinners who repent and turn to Him. God is a compassionate and merciful Father. The parable of the prodigal son, along with the parables of the lost sheep and the lost coin, helps us see and understand the love and desire God has for the lost. It is because of His love for humanity that He sent His only Son, Jesus Christ, to redeem the entire world from death and sin. He sent Jesus for one purpose, and that purpose was to save lost sinners. Jesus did not come for the righteous but for sinners (Mark 2:17).

God is a God of love, mercy, and compassion. He does not want anybody to perish but all to inherit His kingdom. The arrival of the kingdom of heaven here on earth in the person of Jesus marked the arrival of mercy, compassion, love, and forgiveness for all those who humble themselves, repent, and turn to God.

Other Parables

The other parables also teach us important spiritual truths. The parables of the hidden treasure and the priceless pearl illustrate the immense value and importance of the kingdom of God. Because the kingdom is valuable above everything else, we must be willing to give up anything that might hinder us from pursuing it. God's kingdom is worth our life, time, and dedication, for the one who finds God's kingdom finds life and a great treasure.

The parable of the net teaches us that the kingdom of God is like the fisherman's net that catches all kinds of fish, good and bad. However, like the fisherman, who at the end of the day separates the good fish from the bad fish, God will separate the righteous from the wicked on the judgment day. The parable of the net closely parallels the parable of the wheat and the weeds (Matthew 13:24–30, 38–43). It assures us that while we may endure injustice in the present, in God's kingdom justice will be done in due time. The parable encourages us to live a righteous life in the light of the living God and the power of His Holy Spirit.

The parable of the unforgiving servant dramatically and powerfully illustrates God's forgiveness of our many sins and how we must respond by extending forgiveness to others without keeping a record of their wrongs. As kingdom-dwellers, we must follow in the footsteps of our Master, the Lord Jesus Christ, and forgive without any limit those who trespass against us.

The parable of the day laborers, or vineyard workers, teaches us an important principle of God and His kingdom: God is not a respecter of persons. He treats everybody—whether they are new believers in the Lord or mature Christians—equally as His beloved children. Those who are spiritually stronger should never feel superior to new Christians but rather display God's generosity to them. They are equally important to God, and He will reward them according to His grace, the same way

The Parables of the Kingdom

He rewards those who have followed Him for many years. As citizens of God's kingdom, we are to encourage those who are spiritually weak and help them grow in the Lord to the glory and honor of God's name.

The parable of the two sons teaches us the importance of obedience that is carried out in accordance with the Word and will of God. Just saying yes is not enough; we must actually *do* what our Father in heaven tells us to do. Promising obedience to God but not fulfilling our commitment shows how detached we are from Him as our Father. Obedience in the kingdom of God is better than sacrifice (1 Samuel 15:22). When we say yes to God and actually do what He has commanded us to do, we demonstrate to the world and the enemies of the kingdom that we are truly children of the living God.

The parable of the wedding banquet teaches us that God has sent out to all humanity His invitation to dine with Him in His kingdom. However, it is up to each person to accept God's invitation. All are invited to enter God's kingdom, but only those who repent and accept the invitation are chosen to enter. Have you accepted God's invitation?

The parable of the ten virgins, or bridesmaids, teaches us to be ready and prepared for the unannounced and sudden coming of Christ, our bridegroom. No one knows the day or the hour when Jesus Christ will return; so we must be ever vigilant and prepared for His sudden coming. We do not want to risk missing out on meeting the King of kings, like the five foolish bridesmaids who missed out on the wedding banquet. If the Messiah were to come today, would He find you ready or unprepared? Be ready at all times, for the King indeed is coming back.

The parable of the talents helps us understand how we are to live and what we are to do as we await the return of our

Master, Jesus Christ. We are to invest and use every gift God has given us to bear fruit for His kingdom. We are not to hide our God-given abilities and gifts but use them to bring honor and glory to His name and to build up His body, the church.

Conclusion

The kingdom of God, or kingdom of heaven, is a major theme of the New Testament and the primary subject of Jesus' preaching. To fully understand Jesus' teaching on the kingdom of God, however, we must understand His parables, for they reveal the nature, character, and power of God's kingdom. And as we learn the principles of God's kingdom and await the revelation of that kingdom in its fullness at Christ's return, let us apply the spiritual lessons those parables teach so that we might be transformed into godly, obedient servants who will welcome the Lord's return and be welcomed by our Savior into His eternal kingdom.

Bibliography

Beynon, Nigel, and Andrew Sach. *Dig Deeper: Tools for Understanding God's Word*. Wheaton, IL: Good News Publishers, 2010.

Bivin, David, and Roy Blizzard Jr. *Understanding the Difficult Words of Jesus*, revised edition. Shippensburg, PA: Destiny Image, 1994.

Blomberg, Craig L. *Interpreting the Parables*. 2nd edition. Downers Grove, IL: InterVarsity Press, 1990.

Brown, Colin, ed., *The New International Dictionary of New Testament Theology*. 3 vols. Grand Rapids: Zondervan, 1975.

Burge, Gary M. *Jesus the Middle Eastern Storyteller*. Grand Rapids: Zondervan, 2009.

Carson, D. A. "Matthew" in *The Expositor's Bible Commentary*. Vol. 8. Edited by Frank E. Gaebelein. Grand Rapids: Zondervan, 1979.

Curry, Jeffrey L. *The Parable Discovery*. Roanoke, TX: See Again Press, 2004.

Curry, Jeffrey L. *The Mysteries of the Kingdom*. Roanoke, TX: See Again Press, 2004.

Dodd. C. H. *The Parables of the Kingdom*. Glasgow: Collins, 1961.

Dosker, Henry E. "Herod," *The International Standard Bible Encyclopedia*. Edited by James Orr. Grand Rapids: Eerdmans, 1956.

Gray, Steve. *When the Kingdom Comes*. Kansas City: World Revival Press, 1999.

Keener, Craig. *Matthew*. Downers Grove, IL: InterVarsity Press, 1997.

Kissinger, Warren S. *The Parables of Jesus*. Lanham, MD: Scarecrow Press, 1989.

Ladd, George Eldon. *The Gospel of the Kingdom*. Grand Rapids/Cambridge, UK: Eerdmans, 1959; reprinted 2000.

Lundstrom, Gosta. *The Kingdom of God in the Teachings of Jesus*. Richmond: John Knox Press, 1963.

Munroe, Myles. *Rediscovering the Kingdom*. Shippensburg, PA: Destiny Image, 2010.

Phillips, Rob. *The Kingdom according to Jesus*. Bloomington, IN: CrossBooks, 2009.

Tverberg, Lois. *Walking in the Dust of Rabbi Jesus*. Grand Rapids: Zondervan, 2012.

Tverberg, Lois, and Ann Spangler. *Sitting at the Feet of Rabbi Jesus*. Grand Rapids: Zondervan, 2009.

Young, Brad H. *Jesus the Jewish Theologian*. Grand Rapids: Baker Academic, 1995.

Young, Brad H. *The Parables" The Jewish Tradition and Christian Interpretation*. Peabody, MA: Hendrickson, 1998.

CPSIA information can be obtained
at www.ICGtesting.com
Printed in the USA
BVHW042325190620
581826BV00009B/294